Cross-Lingual Word Embeddings

Synthesis Lectures on Human Language Technologies

Editor
Graeme Hirst, *University of Toronto*

Synthesis Lectures on Human Language Technologies is edited by Graeme Hirst of the University of Toronto. The series consists of 50- to 150-page monographs on topics relating to natural language processing, computational linguistics, information retrieval, and spoken language understanding. Emphasis is on important new techniques, on new applications, and on topics that combine two or more HLT subfields.

Cross-Lingual Word Embeddings
Anders Søgaard, Ivan Vulić, Sebastian Ruder, and Manaal Faruqui
2019

Bayesian Analysis in Natural Language Processing, Second Edition
Shay Cohen
2019

Argumentation Mining
Manfred Stede and Jodi Schneider
2018

Quality Estimation for Machine Translation
Lucia Specia, Carolina Scarton, and Gustavo Henrique Paetzold
2018

Natural Language Processing for Social Media, Second Edition
Atefeh Farzindar and Diana Inkpen
2017

Automatic Text Simplification
Horacio Saggion
2017

Neural Network Methods for Natural Language Processing
Yoav Goldberg
2017

Cross-Lingual Word Embeddings

Anders Søgaard, Ivan Vulić, Sebastian Ruder, and Manaal Faruqui

ISBN: 978-3-031-01043-9   paperback
ISBN: 978-3-031-02171-8   ebook
ISBN: 978-3-031-00182-6   hardcover

DOI 10.1007/978-3-031-02171-8

A Publication in the Springer series
SYNTHESIS LECTURES ON HUMAN LANGUAGE TECHNOLOGIES

Lecture #42
Series Editor: Graeme Hirst, *University of Toronto*
Series ISSN
Print 1947-4040   Electronic 1947-4059

Cross-Lingual Word Embeddings

Anders Søgaard
University of Copenhagen

Ivan Vulić
University of Cambridge

Sebastian Ruder
DeepMind

Manaal Faruqui
Google Assistant

SYNTHESIS LECTURES ON HUMAN LANGUAGE TECHNOLOGIES #42

ABSTRACT

The majority of natural language processing (NLP) is English language processing, and while there is good language technology support for (standard varieties of) English, support for Albanian, Burmese, or Cebuano—and most other languages—remains limited. Being able to bridge this digital divide is important for scientific and democratic reasons but also represents an enormous growth potential. A key challenge for this to happen is learning to align basic meaning-bearing units of different languages.

In this book, the authors survey and discuss recent and historical work on supervised and unsupervised learning of such alignments. Specifically, the book focuses on so-called cross-lingual word embeddings. The survey is intended to be systematic, using consistent notation and putting the available methods on comparable form, making it easy to compare wildly different approaches. In so doing, the authors establish previously unreported relations between these methods and are able to present a fast-growing literature in a very compact way. Furthermore, the authors discuss how best to evaluate cross-lingual word embedding methods and survey the resources available for students and researchers interested in this topic.

KEYWORDS

natural language processing, machine learning, semantics, cross-lingual learning

Contents

Preface

In recent decades, we have witnessed an increasing *digital language divide*, that is, large differences in what information and services are accessible to people around the world, depending on their mother tongue. Learning cross-lingual word embeddings facilitates transfer of technologies between languages, narrowing this divide. The last five years has seen a surge in cross-lingual word embedding algorithms, many of which lend intuitions, algorithms, and terminology from neighboring fields, including computer vision, graph theory, and information retrieval. Since these algorithms bring different baggage, they often seem very different at surface level. This book surveys cross-lingual word embedding algorithms and aims to show that many of these algorithms are, in fact, quite similar.

Thanks to our editors and anonymous reviewers for providing helpful feedback on our first draft of this book. Its shortcomings are entirely our fault: The book is intended to be *both* readable by first-year M.Sc. students *and* interesting to an expert audience. Our intention is to introduce what is necessary to appreciate the major challenges we face in cross-lingual NLP, without wasting too much time on fundamentals in linguistic typology, linear algebra, graph theory, or machine learning. In cross-lingual NLP, data is so noisy and biased that few theoretical guarantees can be established, and we are typically left with our gut feelings and a catalog of crazy ideas. We hope this book will provide its readers with both.

Anders Søgaard, Ivan Vulić, Sebastian Ruder, and Manaal Faruqui
May 2019

CHAPTER 1

Introduction

Vector representations of words, so-called *word embeddings* (Mikolov et al., 2013a, Pennington et al., 2014) have become an integral part of the starter's kit for anyone doing Natural Language Processing (NLP). Representing words as vectors rather than discrete variables, at least in theory, enables generalization across syntactically or semantically similar words; and easy-to-implement, easy-to-train word embedding algorithms (Mikolov et al., 2013a, Pennington et al., 2014) have made high-quality word embeddings accessible for most domains and languages.

While monolingual word embeddings can be obtained for most languages, the embeddings are not comparable across languages, hence, cannot be used in multilingual or cross-lingual NLP applications. Multilingual NLP applications range from machine translation and multilingual information retrieval, over language-agnostic text mining, to *universal* syntactic or semantic parsers (Ammar et al., 2016a, Johannsen et al., 2015), trained to exploit the synergies between languages. With the increased public awareness of the digital language divide,[1] many researchers have also begun exploring to what extent NLP models can be transferred across languages. Word embeddings that are comparable across languages—i.e., living in a cross-lingual space as illustrated in Figure 1.1, such that syntactically and semantically similar words in different languages are close—would be a key facilitator for cross-lingual transfer.

Cross-lingual word embeddings are appealing for two reasons.

- First, they enable us *to compare the meaning of words across languages*, which is key to multilingual NLP applications such as bilingual lexicon induction, machine translation, or multilingual information retrieval.

- Second, cross-lingual word embeddings potentially *enable cross-lingual model transfer between languages*, e.g., between resource-rich and low-resource languages, by providing a common representation space. Such transfer can narrow the digital language divide, i.e., the asymmetries in what NLP tools are available across languages.

This dual purpose of cross-lingual word embeddings is also reflected in how they are evaluated, as discussed in Chapter 10.

In this book, we will give a comprehensive overview of existing cross-lingual word embedding models. One of our goals is to show the similarities and differences between these approaches. To facilitate this, we introduce a common notation and terminology at the end of this chapter. Over the course of the book, we show that existing cross-lingual word embedding

---

[1]For example, http://labs.theguardian.com/digital-language-divide/.

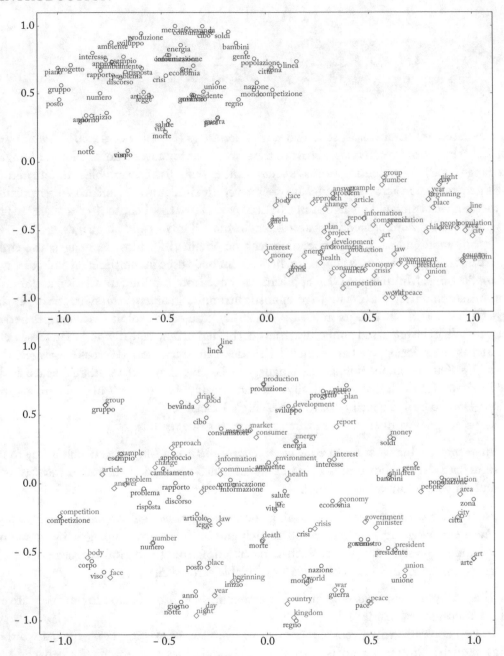

Figure 1.1: Unaligned monolingual word embeddings (left) and word embeddings projected into a joint cross-lingual word embedding space (right) using a method of Smith et al. (2017). Embeddings are visualized with t-SNE (van der Maaten and Hinton, 2012).

models can be seen as optimizing very similar objectives, where the main source of variation is due to the data used, the monolingual and regularization objectives employed, and how these are optimized. As many cross-lingual word embedding models are inspired by monolingual models, we introduce the most commonly used monolingual word embedding models in **Chapter** 2. We then motivate and introduce one of the main contributions of this survey, a typology of *supervised* cross-lingual word embedding models, in **Chapter** 3. The typology is based on the main differentiating aspect of cross-lingual word embedding models: the nature of the data they require, in particular the type of cross-lingual supervision (alignment of words, sentences, or documents), and whether aligned data is assumed to be *parallel*, i.e., translation equivalent, or just *comparable*, i.e., about the same topic. The typology allows us to outline similarities and differences between methods more concisely, but also enables us to identify research directions that have so far gone mostly unexplored.

The idea of cross-lingual representations of words pre-dates the popularization of word embeddings inspired by (deep) neural networks, and we provide a brief overview of the early history of cross-lingual word representations in **Chapter** 4. Subsequent chapters are dedicated to each type of alignment. We discuss cross-lingual word embedding algorithms that rely on word-level alignments in **Chapter** 5. Such methods can be further divided into mapping-based approaches, approaches based on pseudo-mixed corpora, and joint methods. We show that these approaches, *modulo* optimization strategies and hyper-parameters, are nevertheless often equivalent. We then discuss approaches that rely on sentence-level alignments in **Chapter** 6, and models that require document-level alignments in **Chapter** 7. In **Chapter** 8, we then describe how many bilingual approaches can be extended to the multilingual setting. **Chapter** 9 surveys recent work in learning cross-lingual word embeddings in an unsupervised fashion, without relying on *any* explicit bilingual supervision signal.

The development of NLP models is guided by how we evaluate and apply them. We therefore provide an extensive discussion of the tasks, benchmarks, and challenges of the evaluation of cross-lingual word embedding models, as well as a list of their most common applications in **Chapter** 10. **Chapter** 11 lists useful resources for students and others interested in contributing to this field. Finally, we present general challenges and future research directions in learning cross-lingual word embeddings in **Chapter** 12. Throughout the book, we also list some **open problems** which will hopefully motivate researchers to invest more effort and propose new creative solutions in this very vibrant field of representation learning.

In summary, our book is intended to make the following contributions.

1. We propose a general typology that characterizes the differentiating features of cross-lingual word embedding models and provides a compact overview of these models. We hope the typology will be useful for future research, making it easier to relate to previous work.

2. We establish formal relations between three types of word-level alignment models and show that these models are optimizing very similar and sometimes equivalent objectives.

We hope this will inspire more formal work on proving equivalences and mapping out the relations between popular approaches.

3. We discuss the standard ways of evaluating cross-lingual word embedding models, arguing that here, there is some room for improvement.

4. We describe multilingual extensions for the most common types of cross-lingual word embedding models. We believe multilingual word embedding models provide important regularization (and therefore generalize better) compared to strictly bilingual word embedding models.

5. Finally, our book outlines research horizons in cross-lingual learning and provides suggestions for fruitful and unexplored research directions.

Disclaimer   While we do cover historical approaches to cross-lingual word representations, and discuss word alignments a bit, we do not discuss Neural Machine Translation (NMT) models in this book. Most approaches to NMT *implicitly* learn a shared cross-lingual word embedding space by optimizing for Machine Translation (MT) performance, whereas we will focus on models that *explicitly* learn cross-lingual word representations throughout this survey. These methods generally do so at a much lower cost than MT and are sometimes used to pretrain MT models (Artetxe et al., 2018d, Lample et al., 2018a,b).

Notation   For clarity, we show all notation used throughout this survey in Table 1.1. We use bold lowercase letters ($\mathbf{x}$) to denote vectors, bold uppercase letters ($\mathbf{X}$) to denote matrices, and standard weight letters (x) for scalars. We use subscripts with bold letters ($\mathbf{x}_i$) to refer to entire rows or columns and subscripts with standard weight letters for specific elements (x_i).

Let $\mathbf{X}^\ell \in \mathbb{R}^{|V^\ell| \times d}$ be a word embedding matrix that is learned for the ℓ-th of L languages where V^ℓ is the corresponding vocabulary and d is the dimensionality of the word embeddings. We will furthermore refer to the word embedding of the i-th word in language ℓ with the shorthand $\mathbf{x}_i^\ell$ or $\mathbf{x}_i$ if language ℓ is clear from context. We will refer to the word corresponding to the i-th word embedding $\mathbf{x}_i$ as w_i where w_i is a string. To make this correspondence clearer, we will in some settings slightly abuse index notation and use $\mathbf{x}_{w_i}$ to indicate the embedding corresponding to word w_i. We will use i to index words based on their order in the vocabulary V, while we will use k to index words based on their order in a corpus C.

Some monolingual word embedding models use a separate embedding for words that occur in the context of other words. We will use $\tilde{x}_i$ as the embedding of the i-th context word and detail its meaning in the next chapter. Most approaches only deal with two languages, a source language s and a target language t.

Some approaches learn a matrix $\mathbf{W}^{s \rightarrow t}$ that can be used to transform the word embedding matrix $\mathbf{X}^s$ of the source language s to that of the target language t. We will designate such a matrix by $\mathbf{W}^{s \rightarrow t} \in \mathbb{R}^{d \times d}$ and $\mathbf{W}$ if the language pairing is unambiguous. These approaches often use n source words and their translations as seed words. In addition, we will use τ as a function

Table 1.1: Notation used throughout this survey

Symbol	Meaning
$\mathbf{X}$	Word embedding matrix
V	Vocabulary
d	Word embedding dimensionality
$\mathbf{x}_i^{\ell}$ / $\mathbf{x}_i$ / $\mathbf{x}_{w_i}$	Word embedding of the i-th word in language l
$\tilde{x}_i$	Word embedding of the i-th context word
w_i	Word pertaining to embedding $\mathbf{x}_i$
$\mathcal{C}$	Corpus of words / aligned sentences used for training
w_k	The k-th word in a corpus $\mathcal{C}$
s	Source language
t	Target language
$\mathbf{W}^{s \to t}$ / $\mathbf{W}$	Learned transformation matrix between space of s and t
n	Number of words used as seed words for learning $\mathbf{W}$
τ	Function mapping from source words to their translations
$\mathbf{C}^s$	Monolingual co-occurrence matrix in language s
C	Size of context window around a center word
$\mathbf{A}^{s \to t}$	Cross-lingual co-occurrence matrix/alignment matrix
$sent_i^s$	i-th sentence in language s
$\mathbf{y}_i^s$	Representation of i-th sentence in language s
doc_i^s	i-th document in language s
$\mathbf{z}_i^s$	Representation of i-th document in language s
$\underline{\mathbf{X}^s}$	$\mathbf{X}^s$ is kept fixed during optimization
$\underbrace{\mathcal{L}^1}_{1} + \underbrace{\mathcal{L}^2}_{2}$	$\mathcal{L}^1$ is optimized before $\mathcal{L}^2$

that maps from source words w_i^s to their translation w_i^t: $\tau : V^s \to V^t$. Approaches that learn a transformation matrix are usually referred to as *offline*, *mapping*, or *projection-based* methods. As one of the goals of this survey is to standardize nomenclature, we will use the term *mapping* in the following to designate such approaches.

Some approaches require a monolingual word-word co-occurrence matrix $\mathbf{C}^s$ in language s. In such a matrix, every row corresponds to a word w_i^s and every column corresponds to a context word w_j^s. $\mathbf{C}_{ij}^s$ then captures the number of times word w_i occurs with context word w_j

usually within a window of size C to the left and right of word w_i. In a cross-lingual context, we obtain a matrix of alignment counts $\mathbf{A}^{s \rightarrow t} \in \mathbb{R}^{|V^t| \times |V^s|}$, where each element $\mathbf{A}_{ij}^{s \rightarrow t}$ captures the number of times the i−th word in language t was aligned with the j-th word in language s, with each row normalized to sum to 1.

Finally, as some approaches rely on pairs of aligned sentences, we use $sent_1^s, \ldots, sent_n^s$ to designate sentences in source language s with representations $\mathbf{y}_1^s, \ldots, \mathbf{y}_n^s$ where $\mathbf{y} \in \mathbb{R}^d$. We analogously refer to their aligned sentences in the target language t as $sent_1^t, \ldots, sent_n^t$ with representations $\mathbf{y}_1^t, \ldots, \mathbf{y}_n^t$. We adopt an analogous notation for representations obtained by approaches based on alignments of documents in s and t: $doc_1^s, \ldots, doc_n^s$ and $doc_1^t, \ldots, doc_n^t$ with document representations $\mathbf{z}_1^s, \ldots, \mathbf{z}_n^s$ and $\mathbf{z}_1^t, \ldots, \mathbf{z}_n^t$, respectively, where $\mathbf{z} \in \mathbb{R}^d$.

Different notations make similar approaches appear different. Using the same notation across our survey facilitates recognizing similarities between the various cross-lingual word embedding models. Specifically, we intend to demonstrate that cross-lingual word embedding models are trained by minimizing roughly the same objective functions, and that differences in objective are unlikely to explain the observed performance differences (Levy et al., 2017).

The class of objective functions minimized by most cross-lingual word embedding methods (if not all), can be formulated as follows:

$$J = \mathcal{L}^1 + \ldots + \mathcal{L}^\ell + \Omega, \tag{1.1}$$

where $\mathcal{L}^\ell$ is the monolingual loss of the l-th language and Ω is a regularization term. A similar loss was also defined by Upadhyay et al. (2016). As recent work by Levy and Goldberg (2014) and Levy et al. (2015) shows that many monolingual losses are very similar, one of the main contributions of this survey is to condense the difference between approaches into a regularization term and to detail the assumptions that underlie different regularization terms.

Importantly, how this objective function is optimized is a key characteristic and differentiating factor between different approaches. The joint optimization of multiple non-convex losses is difficult. Most approaches thus take a step-wise approach and optimize one loss at a time while keeping certain variables fixed. Such a step-wise approach is approximate as it does not guarantee to reach even a local optimum.[2] In most cases, we will use a longer formulation such as the one below in order to decompose in what order the losses are optimized and which variables they depend on:

$$J = \underbrace{\mathcal{L}(\mathbf{X}^s) + \mathcal{L}(\mathbf{X}^t)}_{1} + \underbrace{\Omega(\underline{\mathbf{X}^s}, \underline{\mathbf{X}^t}, \mathbf{W})}_{2}. \tag{1.2}$$

The underbraces indicate that the two monolingual loss terms on the left, which depend on $\mathbf{X}^s$ and $\mathbf{X}^t$, respectively, are optimized first. Note that this term decomposes into two separate monolingual optimization problems. Subsequently, Ω is optimized, which depends on $\underline{\mathbf{X}^s}, \underline{\mathbf{X}^t}, \mathbf{W}$. Underlined variables are kept fixed during optimization of the corresponding loss.

---

[2]Other strategies such as alternating optimization methods, e.g., the EM algorithm (Dempster et al., 1977) could be used with the same objective.

The monolingual losses are optimized by training one of several monolingual embedding models on a monolingual corpus. These models are outlined in the next chapter.

CHAPTER 2

Monolingual Word Embedding Models

The majority of cross-lingual embedding models take inspiration from and extend monolingual word embedding models to bilingual settings, or explicitly leverage monolingually trained models. As an important preliminary, we thus briefly review monolingual embedding models that have been used in the cross-lingual embeddings literature.

Latent Semantic Analysis (LSA) Latent Semantic Analysis (Deerwester et al., 1990) has been one of the most widely used methods for learning dense word representations. LSA is typically applied to factorize a sparse word-word co-occurrence matrix $\mathbf{C}$ obtained from a corpus. A common preprocessing method is to replace every entry in $\mathbf{C}$ with its pointwise mutual information (PMI) (Church and Hanks, 1990) score:

$$PMI(w_i, w_j) = \log \frac{p(w_i, w_j)}{p(w_i) p(w_j)} = \log \frac{\#(w_i, w_j) \cdot |\mathcal{C}|}{\#(w_i) \cdot \#(w_j)}, \tag{2.1}$$

where $\#(\cdot)$ counts the number of (co-)occurrences in the corpus $\mathcal{C}$. As for unobserved word pairs, $PMI(w_i, w_j) = \log 0 = \infty$, such values are often set to $PMI(w_i, w_j) = 0$, which is also known as positive PMI.

The PMI matrix $\mathbf{P}$ where $\mathbf{P}_{i,j} = PMI(w_i, w_j)$ is then factorized using singular value decomposition (SVD), which decomposes $\mathbf{P}$ into the product of three matrices:

$$\mathbf{P} = \mathbf{U}\mathbf{\Psi}\mathbf{V}^\top, \tag{2.2}$$

where $\mathbf{U}$ and $\mathbf{V}$ are in column orthonormal form and $\mathbf{\Psi}$ is a diagonal matrix of singular values. We subsequently obtain the word embedding matrix $\mathbf{X}$ by reducing the word representations to dimensionality k the following way:

$$\mathbf{X} = \mathbf{U}_k \mathbf{\Psi}_k, \tag{2.3}$$

where $\mathbf{\Psi}_k$ is the diagonal matrix containing the top k singular values and $\mathbf{U}_k$ is obtained by selecting the corresponding columns from $\mathbf{U}$.

Max-margin hinge loss (MMHL) Collobert and Weston (2008) learn word embeddings by training a model on a corpus $\mathcal{C}$ to output a higher score for a correct word sequence than for an incorrect one. For this purpose, they use a max-margin or hinge loss:[1]

$$\mathcal{L}_{\text{MMHL}} = \sum_{k=C+1}^{|\mathcal{C}|-C} \sum_{w' \in V} \max(0, 1 - f([\mathbf{x}_{w_{k-C}}, \dots, \mathbf{x}_{w_i}, \dots, \mathbf{x}_{w_{k+C}}])$$
$$+ f([\mathbf{x}_{w_{k-C}}, \dots, \mathbf{x}_{w'}, \dots, \mathbf{x}_{w_{k+C}}])). \tag{2.4}$$

The outer sum iterates over all words in the corpus $\mathcal{C}$, while the inner sum iterates over all words in the vocabulary. Each word sequence consists of a center word w_k and a window of C words to its left and right. The neural network, which is given by the function $f(\cdot)$, consumes the sequence of word embeddings corresponding to the window of words and outputs a scalar. Using this max-margin loss, it is trained to produce a higher score for a word window occurring in the corpus (the top term) than a word sequence where the center word is replaced by an arbitrary word w' from the vocabulary (the bottom term).

Skip-gram with negative sampling (SGNS)   Skip-gram with negative sampling (Mikolov et al., 2013a) is arguably still the most popular method to learn monolingual word embeddings due to its training efficiency and robustness (Levy et al., 2015). SGNS approximates a language model but focuses on learning efficient word representations rather than accurately modeling word probabilities. It induces representations that are good at predicting surrounding context words given a target word w_k. To this end, it minimizes the negative log-likelihood of the training data under the following *skip-gram* objective:

$$\mathcal{L}_{\text{SGNS}} = -\frac{1}{|\mathcal{C}| - C} \sum_{k=C+1}^{|\mathcal{C}|-C} \sum_{-C \leq j \leq C, j \neq 0} \log P(w_{k+j} \mid w_k), \tag{2.5}$$

$P(w_{k+j} \mid w_k)$ is computed using the softmax function:

$$P(w_{k+j} \mid w_k) = \frac{\exp(\tilde{\mathbf{x}}_{w_{k+j}}^{\top} \mathbf{x}_{w_k})}{\sum_{i=1}^{|V|} \exp(\tilde{\mathbf{x}}_{w_i}^{\top} \mathbf{x}_{w_k})}, \tag{2.6}$$

where $\mathbf{x}_i$ and $\tilde{\mathbf{x}}_i$ are the word and context word embeddings of word w_i, respectively. The skip-gram architecture can be seen as a simple neural network: The network takes as input a one-hot representation of a word $\in \mathbb{R}^{|V|}$ and produces a probability distribution over the vocabulary $\in \mathbb{R}^{|V|}$. The embedding matrix $\mathbf{X}$ and the context embedding matrix $\tilde{X}$ are simply the input-hidden and (transposed) hidden-output weight matrices respectively. The neural network has no nonlinearity, so is equivalent to a matrix product (similar to Equation (2.2)) followed by softmax.

---

[1] Equations in the literature slightly differ in how they handle corpus boundaries. To make comparing between different monolingual methods easier, we define the sum as starting with the $(C + 1)$-th word in the corpus $\mathcal{C}$ (so that the first window includes the first word w_1) and ending with the $(|\mathcal{C}| - C)$-th word (so that the final window includes the last word $w_{|\mathcal{C}|}$).

As the partition function in the denominator of the softmax is expensive to compute, SGNS uses Negative Sampling, which approximates the softmax to make it computationally more efficient. Negative sampling is a simplification of Noise Contrastive Estimation (Gutmann and Hyvärinen, 2012), which was applied to language modeling by Mnih and Teh (2012). Similar to noise contrastive estimation, negative sampling trains the model to distinguish a target word w_k from negative samples drawn from a "noise distribution" P_n. In this regard, it is similar to MML as defined above, which ranks true sentences above noisy sentences. Negative sampling is defined as follows:

$$P(w_{k+j} \mid w_k) = \log \sigma(\tilde{\boldsymbol{x}}_{w_{k+j}}^{\top} \mathbf{x}_{w_k}) + \sum_{i=1}^{N} \mathbb{E}_{w_i \sim P_n} \log \sigma(-\tilde{\boldsymbol{x}}_{w_i}^{\top} \mathbf{x}_{w_k}), \qquad (2.7)$$

where σ is the sigmoid function $\sigma(x) = 1/(1 + e^{-x})$ and N is the number of negative samples. The distribution P_n is empirically set to the unigram distribution raised to the $3/4^{th}$ power. Levy and Goldberg (2014) observe that negative sampling does not in fact minimize the negative log-likelihood of the training data as in Equation (2.5), but rather implicitly factorizes a shifted PMI matrix similar to LSA.

Continuous bag-of-words (CBOW)   While skip-gram predicts each context word separately from the center word, continuous bag-of-words jointly predicts the center word based on all context words. The model receives as input a window of C context words and seeks to predict the target word w_k by minimizing the CBOW objective:

$$\mathcal{L}_{\text{CBOW}} = -\frac{1}{|\mathcal{C}| - C} \sum_{k=C+1}^{|\mathcal{C}|-C} \log P(w_k \mid w_{k-C}, \dots, w_{k-1}, w_{k+1}, \dots, w_{k+C}) \qquad (2.8)$$

$$P(w_k \mid w_{k-C}, \dots, w_{k+C}) = \frac{\exp(\tilde{\boldsymbol{x}}_{w_k}^{\top} \bar{\boldsymbol{x}}_{w_k})}{\sum_{i=1}^{|V|} \exp(\tilde{\boldsymbol{x}}_{w_i}^{\top} \bar{\boldsymbol{x}}_{w_k})}, \qquad (2.9)$$

where $\bar{\boldsymbol{x}}_{w_k}$ is the sum of the word embeddings of the words $w_{k-C}, \dots, w_{k+C}$, i.e., $\bar{\boldsymbol{x}}_{w_k} = \sum_{-C \le j \le C, j \neq 0} \mathbf{x}_{w_{k+j}}$. The CBOW architecture is typically also trained with negative sampling for the same reason as the skip-gram model.

Global vectors (GloVe)   Global vectors (Pennington et al., 2014) allows us to learn word representations via matrix factorization. GloVe minimizes the difference between the dot product of the embeddings of a word $\mathbf{x}_{w_i}$ and its context word $\tilde{\boldsymbol{x}}_{w_j}$ and the logarithm of their number of co-occurrences within a certain window size:[2]

$$\mathcal{L}_{\text{GloVe}} = \sum_{i,j=1}^{|V|} f(\mathbf{C}_{ij})(\mathbf{x}_{w_i}^{\top} \tilde{\boldsymbol{x}}_{w_j} + b_i + \tilde{b}_j - \log \mathbf{C}_{ij})^2, \qquad (2.10)$$

---

[2]GloVe favors slightly larger window sizes (up to 10 words to the right and to the left of the target word) compared to SGNS (Levy et al., 2015).

where b_i and $\tilde{b}_j$ are the biases corresponding to word w_i and word w_j, $\mathbf{C}_{ij}$ captures the number of times word w_i occurs with word w_j, and $f(\cdot)$ is a weighting function that assigns relatively lower weight to rare and frequent co-occurrences. If we fix $b_i = \log \#(w_i)$ and $\tilde{b}_j = \log \#(w_j)$, then GloVe is equivalent to factorizing a PMI matrix, shifted by $\log |\mathcal{C}|$ (Levy et al., 2015). We refer to the loss functions in Equations (2.4), (2.5), (2.8), and (2.10) as $\mathcal{L}_{\text{MMHL}}$, $\mathcal{L}_{\text{SGNS}}$, $\mathcal{L}_{\text{CBOW}}$, and $\mathcal{L}_{\text{GloVe}}$, respectively, throughout the remainder of this book.

One final monolingual word embedding algorithm that will be relevant later in this book, is fastText (Bojanowski et al., 2017): this algorithm is trained using $\mathcal{L}_{\text{SGNS}}$ over character n-grams and represents words by their average character n-gram embedding.

CHAPTER 3

Cross-Lingual Word Embedding Models: Typology

This chapter introduces the two most important dimensions of our typology of supervised approaches to learning cross-lingual word embeddings: the type of alignment required for supervision, and the comparability these alignments encode. Unsupervised approaches are discussed in Chapter 9, and we show that they are very similar to supervised approaches, with the only core difference being how they obtain and gradually enrich the required bilingual supervision signal. Focusing on these two dimensions means that, unlike most such typologies in NLP, we initially ignore algorithmic differences between the various approaches and focus on data requirements instead.

This choice does not come out of the blue: Levy et al. (2017) suggest that the choice of bilingual supervision signal—that is, the data used to learn the cross-lingual representation space—is more important for the final model performance than the actual underlying model architecture; see also the empirical evaluations presented in Upadhyay et al. (2016). In other words, large differences between various approaches and how they perform, stem more from the type (and amount) of data used, rather than algorithmic differences, hyper-parameters, and additional tricks and fine-tuning employed. Levy et al. (2015) make a similar point about monolingual word embedding models: They observe that the architecture is less important as long as the models are trained under identical conditions on the same type (and amount) of data.

Instead of algorithmic differences, we base our typology on the data requirements of the cross-lingual word embedding methods, as this accounts for much of the variation in performance. In our typology, methods differ with regard to the data they employ along the following two dimensions.

1. **Type of alignment**: Methods use different types of bilingual supervision signals—at the level of words, sentences, or documents. Some supervision signals are more fine-grained and may, for instance, inform us that two words are meaning equivalent or similar in their respective contexts; but sometimes we have to rely on more coarse-grained signals, aligning similar sentences, or documents.

2. **Comparability**: Methods require either *parallel* data sources, i.e., exact translations in different languages, or *comparable* data that is only similar in some way. In parallel data, there is an approximate one-to-one meaning equivalence between words or sentences; in

comparable data, there is no such meaning equivalence, but an approximate one-to-one correspondence between similar words, sentences, or documents, e.g., documents that are about the same topic. The most widely used source of comparable data is Wikipedia, where we can easily extract documents (pages) about the same topic in multiple languages.

In particular, there are three different levels at which alignments can be defined. We discuss the typical data sources for both parallel and comparable data based on the following alignment signals.

1. **Word alignment**: Most approaches use parallel word-aligned data in the form of a bilingual or cross-lingual dictionary with pairs of synonymous words in different languages (Faruqui and Dyer, 2014, Mikolov et al., 2013b) or in the form of high-precision word alignments. Comparable word-aligned data has been leveraged less often and typically involves other modalities such as images (Bergsma and Van Durme, 2011, Kiela et al., 2015). In general, most approaches we would classify as using word-level comparability for supervision would involve extra-linguistic modalities, such as time of utterance (Cocos and Callison-Burch, 2017) or gaze (Barrett et al., 2016), but one notable exception is the use of parts of speech as a similarity measure in Gouws and Søgaard (2015). Unsupervised cross-lingual word embedding methods also fall into this category: their goal is to extract seed word-aligned data from monolingual corpora and then rely on some of the standard word-level approaches to cross-lingual embedding induction.

2. **Sentence alignment**: Sentence alignment requires a parallel corpus, as commonly used in MT. There has been some work on extracting parallel data from comparable corpora (Munteanu and Marcu, 2006), but no-one has so far trained cross-lingual word embeddings on such data. Comparable data with sentence alignment may again leverage another modality, such as captions of the same image or similar images in different languages, which are not translations of each other (Calixto et al., 2017, Gella et al., 2017).

3. **Document alignment**: Parallel document-aligned data requires documents in different languages that are translations of each other. This is a rare data requirement for cross-lingual word embedding algorithms, as parallel documents typically means sentences can be aligned (Hermann and Blunsom, 2014). Comparable document-aligned data is more common and can occur in the form of documents that are topic-aligned (e.g., Wikipedia) or class-aligned (e.g., sentiment analysis and multi-class classification datasets) (Mogadala and Rettinger, 2016, Vulić and Moens, 2013).

We note that parallel data with meaning equivalence between documents typically involves meaning equivalence between sentences; and, to the best of our knowledge, there have been no approaches to learning cross-lingual word embeddings relying on document-level alignments between meaning-equivalent documents. The five remaining combinations are summarized by the following table.

	Parallel	Comparable
Word	Dictionaries	Images
Sentence	Translations	Captions
Document	-	Wikipedia

Some approaches rely on parallel words (word alignments or dictionary seeds) or parallel sentences (aligned sentences that are assumed to be translations of each other); others rely on comparable words or sentences, i.e., words or sentences used in similar contexts, or comparable documents, e.g., documents about the same topics. We provide examples for each in Figure 3.1.

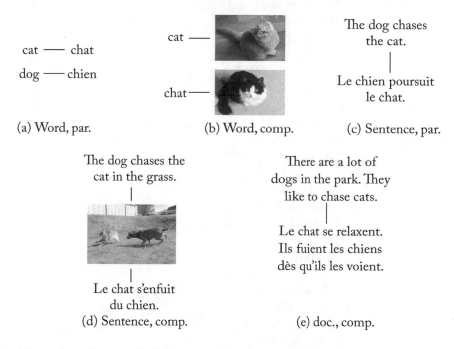

Figure 3.1: Examples of types of alignment of data sources. (Par.: parallel. Comp.: comparable. Doc.: document.) Left to right, top to bottom, word-level parallel alignment in the form of a bilingual lexicon (a), word-level comparable alignment using images obtained with Google search queries (b), sentence-level parallel alignment with translations (c), sentence-level comparable alignment using translations of several image captions (d), and document-level comparable alignment using similar documents (e).

In this book, we will show that models that use a particular type of data are mostly variations of the same or similar architectures. We present our complete typology of cross-lingual word embedding models in Tables 3.1 and 3.2, aiming to provide an exhaustive overview by

Table 3.1: Cross-lingual embedding models ordered by data requirements. Part 1: Methods that leverage word-level alignment.

		Parallel	Comparable
Word	Mapping	Mikolov et al. (2013) Faruqui and Dyer (2014) Lazaridou et al. (2015) Dinu et al. (2015) Xing et al. (2015) Lu et al. (2015) Vulic and Korhonen (2016) Ammar et al. (2016) Zhang et al. (2016, 2017ab) Artexte et al. (2016, 2017, 2018ab) Smith et al. (2017) Hauer et al. (2017) Mrkšic et al. (2017) Nakashole and Flauger (2017) Wijaya et al. (2017) Conneau et al. (2018) Joulin et al. (2018) Doval et al. (2018) Hoshen and Wolf (2018) Alvarez-Melis and Jaakkola (2018) Mukherjee et al. (2018) Chen and Cardie (2018) Nakashole (2018) Xu et al. (2018) Dou et al. (2018) Kim et al. (2018) Ruder et al. (2018) Glavaš et al. (2019) Alaux et al. (2018)	Bergsma and Van Durme (2011) Kiela et al. (2015) Vulić et al. (2016)
	Pseudo-bilingual	Xiao and Guo (2014) Gouws and Søgaard (2015) Duong et al. (2016) Adams et al. (2017)	Gouws and Søgaard (2015) Duong et al. (2015)
	Joint	Klementiev et al. (2012) Kociský et al. (2014)	

Table 3.2: Cross-lingual embedding models ordered by data requirements. Part 2: Methods that leverage other types of alignment (beyond words).

		Parallel	Comparable
Sentence	Matrix Factorization	Zou et al. (2013) Shi et al. (2015) Gardner et al. (2015) Guo et al. (2015) Vyas and Carpuat (2016)	
	Compositional	Hermann and Blunsom (2013, 2014) Soyer et al. (2015)	
	Autoencoder	Lauly et al. (2013) Chandar et al. (2014)	
	Skip-gram	Gouws et al. (2015) Luong et al. (2015) Coulmance et al. (2015) Pham et al. (2015)	
	Other	Levy et al. (2017) Rajendran et al. (2016) Dufter et al. (2018)	Calixto et al. (2017) Gella et al. (2017) Rotman et al. (2018)
Document			Vulic and Moens (2013, 2014, 2016) Søgaard et al. (2015) Mogadala and Rettinger (2016)

classifying each model (we are aware of) into one of the corresponding model types. Table 3.1 lists approaches based on word-level alignment: as the table suggests, these methods have become predominant in the most recent work, with a particular focus on projection-based methods. Table 3.2 lists approaches that require other types of supervision.

We also provide a more detailed overview of the monolingual objectives and regularization terms used by every approach in Table 3.3. The objectives and regularization terms will be discussed in the following sections. The table is meant to reveal—at a glance—the *high-level* objectives and losses each model is optimizing. It also indicates for each method whether all objectives are jointly optimized; if they are, both monolingual losses and regularization terms are optimized jointly; otherwise the monolingual losses are optimized first and the monolingual variables are frozen, while the cross-lingual regularization constraint is optimized. The table obscures smaller differences and implementation details, which can be found in the corresponding sections of this survey or by consulting the original papers. We use Ω_∞ to represent an infinitely

Table 3.3: Overview of approaches with monolingual objectives and regularization terms, with an indication whether the order of optimization matters and short descriptions. Ω_∞ represents an infinitely strong regularizer that enforces equality between representations. * implies that the regularization is achieved in the limit. (*Continues.*)

Approach	Monolingual	Regularizer	Joint	Description
Klementiev et al. (2012)	$\mathcal{L}_{\text{MLE}}$	Ω_{MSE}	✓	Joint
Mikolov et al. (2013)	$\mathcal{L}_{\text{SGNS}}$	Ω_{MSE}		Projection-based
Zou et al. (2013)	$\mathcal{L}_{\text{MMHL}}$	Ω_{MSE}	✓	Matrix factorization
Hermann and Blunsom (2013)	$\mathcal{L}_{\text{MMHL}}$	Ω_{MSE}^*	✓	Sentence-level, joint
Hermann and Blunsom (2014)	$\mathcal{L}_{\text{MMHL}}$	Ω_{MSE}^*	✓	Sentence-level + bigram composition
Soyer et al. (2015)	$\mathcal{L}_{\text{MMHL}}$	Ω_{MSE}^*		Phrase-level
Shi et al. (2015)	$\mathcal{L}_{\text{MMHL}}$	Ω_{MSE}	✓	Matrix factorization
Dinu et al. (2015)	$\mathcal{L}_{\text{SGNS}}$	Ω_{MSE}		Better neighbour retrieval
Gouws et al. (2015)	$\mathcal{L}_{\text{SGNS}}$	Ω_{MSE}	✓	Sentence-level
Vyas and Carpuat (2016)	$\mathcal{L}_{\text{GloVe}}$	Ω_{MSE}		Sparse matrix factorization
Hauer et al. (2017)	$\mathcal{L}_{\text{SGNS}}$	Ω_{MSE}		Cognates
Mogadala and Rettinger (2016)	$\mathcal{L}_{\text{SGNS-P}}$	Ω_{MSE}		Elastic net, Procrustes analysis
Xing et al. (2015)	$\mathcal{L}_{\text{SGNS}}$	Ω_{MSE} s.t.$\mathbf{W}^\top\mathbf{W} = \mathbf{I}$		Normalization, orthogonality
Zhang et al. (2016)	$\mathcal{L}_{\text{SGNS}}$	Ω_{MSE} s.t.$\mathbf{W}^\top\mathbf{W} = \mathbf{I}$		Orthogonality constraint
Artexte et al. (2016)	$\mathcal{L}_{\text{SGNS}}$	Ω_{MSE} s.t.$\mathbf{W}^\top\mathbf{W} = \mathbf{I}$		Normalization, orthogonality, mean centering
Smith et al. (2017)	$\mathcal{L}_{\text{SGNS}}$	Ω_{MSE} s.t.$\mathbf{W}^\top\mathbf{W} = \mathbf{I}$		Orthogonality, inverted softmax identical character strings
Artexte et al. (2017)	$\mathcal{L}_{\text{SGNS}}$	Ω_{MSE} s.t.$\mathbf{W}^\top\mathbf{W} = \mathbf{I}$		Normalization, orthogonality, mean centering, bootstrapping
Lazaridou et al. (2015)	$\mathcal{L}_{\text{CBOW}}$	Ω_{MMHL}		Max-margin with intruders
Mrkšić et al. (2017)	$\mathcal{L}_{\text{SGNS}}$	Ω_{MMHL}		Semantic specialization
Calixto et al. (2017)	$\mathcal{L}_{\text{RNN}}$	Ω_{MMHL}	✓	Image-caption pairs
Gella et al. (2017)	$\mathcal{L}_{\text{RNN}}$	Ω_{MMHL}	✓	Image-caption pairs
Faruqui and Dyer (2014)	$\mathcal{L}_{\text{LSA}}$	Ω_{CCA}		-
Lu et al. (2015)	$\mathcal{L}_{\text{LSA}}$	Ω_{CCA}		Neural CCA
Rajendran et al. (2016)	$\mathcal{L}_{\text{AUTO}}$	Ω_{CCA}		Pivots
Ammar et al. (2016)	$\mathcal{L}_{\text{LSA}}$	Ω_{CCA}		Multilingual CCA
Søgaard et al. (2015)	-	Ω_{SVD}	✓	Inverted indexing
Levy et al. (2017)	$\mathcal{L}_{\text{PMI}}$	Ω_{SVD}	✓	
Levy et al. (2017)	-	Ω_{SGNS}	✓	Inverted indexing
Lauly et al. (2013)	$\mathcal{L}_{\text{AUTO}}$	Ω_{AUTO}	✓	Autoencoder
Chandar et al. (2014)	$\mathcal{L}_{\text{AUTO}}$	Ω_{AUTO}	✓	Autoencoder

Table 3.3: (*Continued.*) Overview of approaches with monolingual objectives and regularization terms, with an indication whether the order of optimization matters and short descriptions. Ω_∞ represents an infinitely strong regularizer that enforces equality between representations. * implies that the regularization is achieved in the limit.

Vulić and Moens (2013a)	$\mathcal{L}_{\text{LDA}}$	Ω_∞^*	✓	Document-level
Vulić and Moens (2014)	$\mathcal{L}_{\text{LDA}}$	Ω_∞^*	✓	Document-level
Xiao and Guo (2014)	$\mathcal{L}_{\text{MMHL}}$	Ω_∞	✓	Pseudo-mixed
Gouws and Søgaard (2015)	$\mathcal{L}_{\text{CBOW}}$	Ω_∞^*	✓	Pseudo-mixed
Luong et al. (2015)	$\mathcal{L}_{\text{SGNS}}$	Ω_∞^*		Monotonic alignment
Gardner et al. (2015)	$\mathcal{L}_{\text{LSA}}$	Ω_∞^*		Matrix factorization
Pham et al. (2015)	$\mathcal{L}_{\text{SGNS-P}}$	Ω_∞	✓	Paragraph vectors
Guo et al. (2015)	$\mathcal{L}_{\text{CBOW}}$	Ω_∞		Weighted by word alignments
Coulmance et al. (2015)	$\mathcal{L}_{\text{SGNS}}$	Ω_∞^*	✓	Sentence-level
Ammar et al. (2016)	$\mathcal{L}_{\text{SGNS}}$	Ω_∞	✓	Pseudo-mixed
Vulić and Korhonen (2016)	$\mathcal{L}_{\text{SGNS}}$	Ω_∞		Highly reliable seed entries
Duong et al. (2016)	$\mathcal{L}_{\text{CBOW}}$	Ω_∞	✓	Pseudo-mixed, polysemy
Vulić and Moens (2016)	$\mathcal{L}_{\text{SGNS}}$	Ω_∞	✓	Pseudo-mixed
Adams et al. (2017)	$\mathcal{L}_{\text{CBOW}}$	Ω_∞	✓	Pseudo-multilingual, polysemy
Bergsma and Van Durme (2011)	–	–	✓	SIFT image features, similarity
Kiela et al. (2015)	–	–	✓	CNN image features, similarity
Vulić et al. (2016)	–	–	✓	CNN features, similarity, inter-polation
Gouws and Søgaard (2015)	$\mathcal{L}_{\text{CBOW}}$	POS-level Ω_∞^*	✓	Pseudo-mixed
Duong et al. (2015)	$\mathcal{L}_{\text{CBOW}}$	POS-level Ω_∞^*	✓	Pseudo-multilingual

stronger regularizer that enforces equality between representations. Regularizers with a * imply that the regularization is achieved in the limit, e.g., in the pseudo-mixed case, where examples are randomly sampled with some equivalence, we obtain the same representation in the limit, without strictly enforcing it to be the same representation.

As we will demonstrate throughout this book, most approaches can be seen as optimizing a combination of monolingual losses with a regularization term. As we can see, some approaches do not employ a regularization term; notably, a small number of approaches, i.e., those that ground language in images, do not optimize a loss but rather use pre-trained image features and a set of similarity heuristics to retrieve translations.

We do not show unsupervised approaches in Table 3.3: this is simply because unsupervised approaches closely follow the paradigm of projection-based word-level approaches, where the only core difference is the use of iterative self-learning and the manner in which seed bilingual dictionaries are extracted and enriched. Their monolingual objectives and regularizers closely resemble the ones from projection-based methods such as the ones formulated by the general framework of Artetxe et al. (2018a), which will be discussed in Chapter 5.

CHAPTER 4

A Brief History of Cross-Lingual Word Representations

We now provide an overview of the historical lineage of cross-lingual word embedding models. In short, while cross-lingual word embeddings at first sight seem like a novel phenomenon in representation learning, many of the high-level ideas that motivate current research in this area can be found in work that pre-dates the popular introduction of word embeddings inspired by neural networks. This includes work on learning cross-lingual clusters and cross-lingual word representations from seed lexicons, parallel data, or document-aligned data, as well as ideas on learning with limited or no bilingual supervision. In what follows, we will briefly survey such "pre-embedding" cross-lingual representation methods and draw direct links to current state-of-the-art representation methodology.

Language-independent representations have been proposed for decades, many of which rely on orthographic features or abstract linguistic features, such as part of speech, instead of lexical features (Aone and McKee, 1993, Schultz and Waibel, 2001). This is also the strategy used in so-called *delexicalized* approaches to cross-lingual model transfer (Cohen et al., 2011, Henderson et al., 2014, McDonald et al., 2011, Søgaard, 2011, Täckström et al., 2012, Zeman and Resnik, 2008), as well as in work on inducing cross-lingual word clusters (Faruqui and Dyer, 2013, Täckström et al., 2012) and cross-lingual word embeddings relying on syntactic/POS contexts (Dehouck and Denis, 2017, Duong et al., 2015).

The ability to represent lexical items from two different languages in a shared cross-lingual vector space also supplements delexicalized cross-lingual transfer by providing fine-grained word-level links between languages; see work in cross-lingual dependency parsing (Ammar et al., 2016a, Zeman et al., 2017) and natural language understanding systems (Mrkšić et al., 2017). The introduction of finer-grained cross-lingual word embeddings into the cross-lingual transfer models can be seen as *relexicalization*: instead of resorting to higher and coarser-grained levels of abstraction such as cross-lingual clusters, the relexicalized models based on cross-lingual word embeddings operate directly with cross-lingual word-level features. Two examples of such relexicalized cross-lingual transfer are shown in Figure 4.1, focused on two standard tasks: (1) cross-lingual document classification; and (2) cross-lingual dependency parsing. The basic transfer idea is exactly the same: the model is trained on a resource-abundant source language where suf-

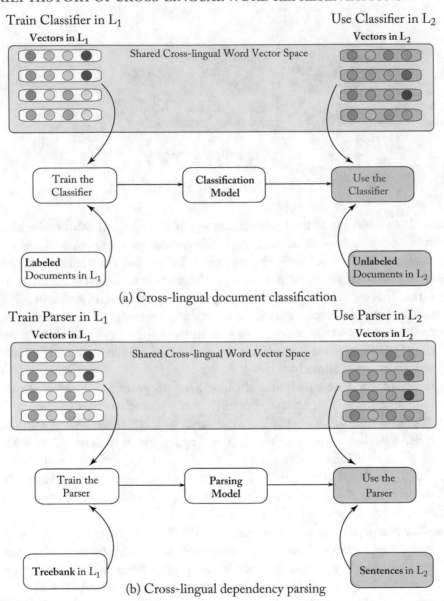

Figure 4.1: A high-level illustration of (relexicalized) cross-lingual transfer methodology powered by cross-lingual word embeddings for (a) document classification and (b) dependency parsing. A pre-trained shared cross-lingual word embedding space is used as the main source of lexical features linking the two languages. Older delexicalization-based models replace the shared embedding space with a coarser-grained language-independent feature set such as cross-lingual cluster labels or universal POS tags.

ficient annotated training data exists, and it is supplemented by the source language subspace of the entire shared cross-lingual embedding space. After training, the model is directly applied to the target language, but now relying on the target language embedding subspace as a feature set. A very similar method for cross-lingual dependency parser transfer operates with cross-lingual word clusters induced from monolingual and sentence-aligned parallel data (Faruqui and Dyer, 2013, Täckström et al., 2012). The method is illustrated in Figure 4.2. The only high-level modeling difference compared to the transfer methodology outlined in Figure 4.1 is the dependence on cross-lingual word clusters instead of cross-lingual word embeddings.

Shared cross-lingual clusters could be seen as discrete groupings of lexical items from two different languages so that semantically related items end up in similar clusters. In monolingual scenarios, clusters are typically based on distributional information coded into a class-based language model (Brown et al., 1992, Uszkoreit and Brants, 2008). Under the hard clustering assumption, the clustering function $\mathcal{F} : V \rightarrow 1, \dots, K$ maps each vocabulary word to exactly one of the K classes/clusters. Probabilities of words are based on the classes (i.e., clusters) of preceding words. The main purpose of clustering is to reduce data sparsity inherent to language modeling. Grouping semantically related words into hard clusters can be seen as a naïve approach to word representation induction which is less expressive than dense real-valued word embeddings: instead of a d-dimensional vector each word is assigned a cluster number. Note that, similar to word clusters, word embeddings also have their roots in the idea of reducing data sparsity for language modeling (Bengio et al., 2003).

In cross-lingual scenarios, the idea remains the same. One learns the clustering function $\mathcal{F} : V^s \sqcup V^t \rightarrow 1, \dots, K$ which groups semantically related words into hard clusters irrespective of their actual language, as shown in the top right corner of Figure 4.1. The cross-lingual grouping is typically achieved either: (1) by a projection method that first clusters the source language vocabulary and then projects the clusters into the target language using bilingual word similarity (Och, 1999) or word alignments (Täckström et al., 2012) estimated from sentence-aligned parallel data; or (2) by maximizing the joint monolingual and bilingual clustering objective (Faruqui and Dyer, 2013, Täckström et al., 2012). For the latter, the bilingual objective again encodes some notion of bilingual word similarity extracted from sentence-aligned data and acts as cross-lingual regularization. Note that the former approach is extremely similar to the cross-lingual word embedding model of Zou et al. (2013), while the latter approach (on a high level) takes the form of joint approaches to cross-lingual embedding learning from word-level and sentence-level supervision, discussed later in Sections 5.1.3 and 6.1.

This direct relationship between (cross-lingual) word clustering and word embedding learning already points at many other high-level similarities between older work in NLP and representation learning, which are briefly reviewed in what follows.

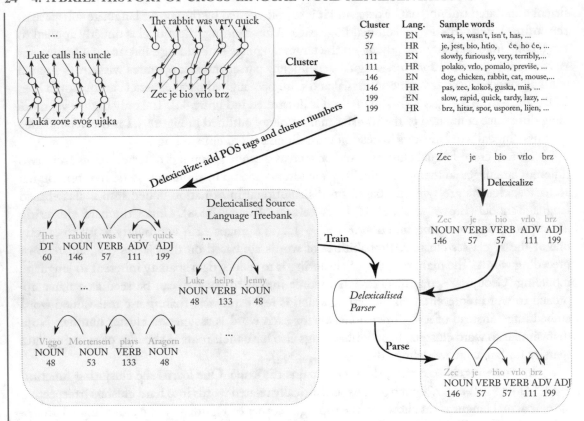

Figure 4.2: Cross-lingual word clusters as features for parser transfer. After the initial cross-lingual clustering step (top) of English (EN) and Croatian (HR) words, cluster numbers and POS tags are used to convert the sentences from the source language EN treebank into delexicalized language-independent representations (lower left). Bottom right: trained cluster-augmented delexicalized parser can be directly applied to parse target language sentences (after their delexicalization). The illustration is based on the work of Täckström et al. (2012). We can replace cross-lingual word clusters with cross-lingual word embeddings within the same framework (cf. Figure 4.1).

4.1 CROSS-LINGUAL WORD REPRESENTATIONS USING BILINGUAL LEXICONS

Other older cross-lingual representation architectures can also be arranged into the same categories we used in Tables 3.1 and 3.2. We start from a traditional approach to cross-lingual vector space induction in distributional semantics. The approach is based on high-dimensional context-counting vectors where each dimension encodes the (weighted) co-occurrences with a specific context word in each of the languages. It relies on the assumption that if two words are mutual translations, then their neighboring words found frequently in their local neighborhoods are also likely to be semantically similar. In short, each word is represented by a high-dimensional vector called *context vector* in a feature vector space (i.e., a semantic space), where the dimensions of the vector are its *context features*. The semantic similarity of two words in the shared semantic space, w_1^s from the source language L_s with vocabulary V^s and w_2^t in the target language L_t is then computed as follows:

$$sim(w_1^s, w_2^t) = SM(vec(w_1^s), vec(w_2^t)), \qquad \cdot \qquad (4.1)$$

where $vec(w_1^s)$ is an N-dimensional context vector with N context features c_n:

$$vec(w_1^s) = [sc_1^s(c_1), \ldots, sc_1^s(c_n), \ldots, sc_1^s(c_N)] \qquad (4.2)$$

$sc_1^s(c_n)$ denotes a co-occurrence weight/score for w_1^s associated with the context feature c_n (similar for w_2^t). SM is a similarity measure operating on the sparse vectors (e.g., cosine similarity, Euclidean distance). Note that the formulation of semantic similarity provided in Equations (4.1) and (4.2) is very general and is also applicable to cross-lingual word embeddings. The difference, however, is in the way vectors $vec(w)$ are created: with traditional context-counting approaches, those are sparse N-dimensional weighted co-occurrence vectors, where N equals the size of the seed bilingual lexicon.

Each dimension of the vector $sc_1^S(c_n)$ assigns a co-occurrence score of the word w_1^s with some context feature c_n. The context scope is predefined and the typical choice is a local bag-of-words neighborhood, as used previously in the monolingual SGNS and CBOW embedding models. Distributional models differ in the way each c_n is weighted, that is, the way the co-occurrence of w_1^s and its context feature c_n is mapped to the score $sc_1^s(c_n)$. There exist a variety of options for weighting: the values of $sc_1^s(c_n)$ can be raw co-occurrence counts $C(w_1^s, c_n)$, conditional feature probability scores $P(c_n|w_1^s)$, weighting heuristics such as term frequency-inverse document frequency (TF-IDF), (positive) point-wise mutual information (PMI and PPMI), or association scores based on hypothesis testing such as log-likelihood ratio (Gaussier et al., 2004, Laroche and Langlais, 2010).

In order to construct a shared cross-lingual semantic space, word representations in two languages have to be computed over the same set of features irrespective of their actual language. A standard approach is to use seed bilingual lexicon entries, i.e., the context features c_n, $n = 1, \ldots, N$ are actually word pairs (c_n^s, c_n^t), where c_n^s is a source language word and c_n^t a target language word which refer to the same concept (e.g., *(dog, perro), (bone, hueso), (blue, azul)*). For each source language word from the source vocabulary V^s, we actually compute its co-occurrence score $sc^s(c_n)$ (in a predefined local context window) with source language words c_n^s present in the seed lexicon. The same process is followed in the target language. Different flavors of the same idea exist in the literature (Fung and Yee, 1998, Gaussier et al., 2004, Laroche and Langlais, 2010, Rapp, 1999, Tamura et al., 2012, inter alia), crucially differing in the choice

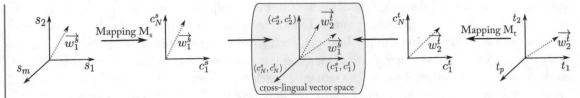

Figure 4.3: Geometric view of the traditional "context-counting" approach to cross-lingual word vector space construction using a seed bilingual lexicon. Initial m-dimensional and p-dimensional monolingual vectors are obtained by weighting co-occurrence with m source language context words (and p target language context words). The vectors on both sides are then mapped to a subspace spanned by N cross-lingual context features $c_n = (c_n^s, c_n^t)$ that occur in the provided seed bilingual lexicon. M_s and M_t are the two projection matrices. The illustration is based on the geometric interpretation of the traditional approach by Gaussier et al. (2004).

of the weighting function and the procedure used to extract the initial seed lexicon (e.g., using readily available lexicons, word alignments from parallel data, or unsupervised methods based on identically spelled words).

The additional requirement, when compared to standard monolingual context-counting representation models (Turney and Pantel, 2010), is the seed bilingual lexicon. The coverage of lexicon limits (or extends) the expressiveness of the model. In fact, in the cross-lingual scenario, the vectors are reduced by replacing monolingual context features with a subset of features that occur in the seed lexicon. This could be seen as *mapping* monolingual vectors into a single cross-lingual space using a seed bilingual dictionary containing paired context words from both sides, as illustrated in Figure 4.3.

Relying on the idea of mapping through a seed bilingual lexicon, this approach is an important predecessor to the cross-lingual word embedding models described in Chapter 5. Further, as the critical requirement is a seed bilingual lexicon, the bootstrapping iterative techniques for gradual enrichment of seed bilingual lexicons were developed for traditional context-counting approaches (Peirsman and Padó, 2010, Vulić and Moens, 2013). The main idea, as illustrated in Figure 4.4, is to add new entries to the lexicon if and only if they pass certain reliability tests (e.g., two words are mutual translations or have a similarity score above a pre-defined threshold). These models are important predecessors to recent unsupervised and weakly supervised iterative self-learning techniques used to limit the bilingual dictionary seed supervision needed in mapping-based approaches (Artetxe et al., 2017, 2018b, Conneau et al., 2018, Hauer et al., 2017), discussed later in Chapter 9.

Further, the idea of CCA-based word embedding learning (see later in Chapter 5) (Faruqui and Dyer, 2014, Lu et al., 2015) was also introduced a decade earlier (Haghighi et al., 2008); their work additionally discussed the idea of combining orthographic subword features with distributional signatures for cross-lingual representation learning. This idea re-entered the

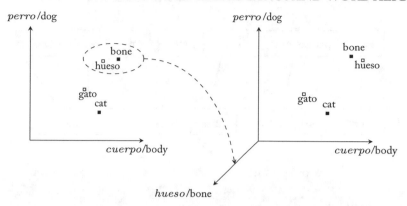

Figure 4.4: An illustration of the bootstrapping approach to constructing a shared Spanish-English cross-lingual vector space. With traditional models, the dimensionality N of the vector space is increased with each entry added to the seed bilingual lexicon. With mapping-based embedding approaches, we expand the training dictionary used to train a mapping function from the source language space to the target language space (cf. Chapter 5), but the dimensionality of the space remains intact.

literature recently (Heyman et al., 2017, Ruder et al., 2018), only now with much better performance.

4.2 CROSS-LINGUAL WORD EMBEDDINGS AND WORD ALIGNMENTS

Cross-lingual word embeddings can also be linked with the work on word alignment[1] for statistical machine translation (Brown et al., 1993, Och and Ney, 2003), and in fact some embedding models (Kočiský et al., 2014, Luong et al., 2015) directly depend on word alignments. In general terms, word alignment is the task of identifying translation relationships among lexical units (typically words) in a sentence-aligned parallel corpus. The final product of a word alignment algorithm is a bipartite graph between the source and the target text: a link between two words exists if and only if they are translations of one another, as illustrated in Figure 4.5.

The series of increasingly complex IBM alignment models (IBM Model 1-6) (Brown et al., 1993, Och and Ney, 2003) are still an algorithmic mainstay in word alignment learning, and they have been used as a crucial component of statistical machine translation (SMT) systems before the dawn of neural MT. The principles behind the simplest IBM Model 1 are often found in cross-lingual word embedding algorithms. In short, IBM Model 1 is based purely on lexical

---

[1]Note the similarity in terminology to avoid confusion: *word alignments* refer to the concept from Statistical Machine Translation, while *word-level alignment* refers to the supervision signal used by several models to learn cross-lingual word embedding; see Chapter 5.

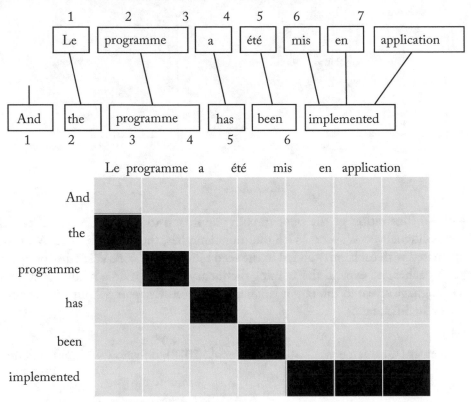

Figure 4.5: A plausible word alignment for an aligned English-French sentence pair. Word alignment models are able to learn that, *(le, the)* or *(programme, programme)*, for example, are likely English-French word translation pairs.

translation, and the crucial set of parameters concerns the so-called *translation tables*: they store probability scores $P(w^t|w^s)$, a probability that a source language word w^s will get translated to a language word w^t. The main (simplifying) assumption of IBM Model 1 is that all of possible $(n_s + 1)^{n^t}$ word alignments are equally likely, where n^s and n^t are the respective lengths of the source and the target sentence from an aligned sentence pair. The parameters of the model (i.e., translation tables) are then learned using an Expectation-Maximization algorithm based on word co-occurrence in aligned sentences, again stressing the initial assumption of all alignments being equally likely (Brown et al., 1993). Higher-order IBM models introduced improvements to IBM Model 1 such as modeling reordering (IBM Model 2) or fertility (IBM Model 3). The main word alignment algorithms are readily available online in packages such as Giza++ (Och and Ney, 2003)[2] from the Moses SMT toolkit, FastAlign (Dyer et al., 2013),[3] cdec (Dyer et al., 2010),[4] and the Berkeley aligner (Liang et al., 2006).[5]

Levy et al. (2017) point that such translation tables with probability scores $P(w^t|w^s)$ extracted from sentence-aligned parallel data by IBM alignment models, other similar word alignment models (Lardilleux et al., 2013, Vulić and Moens, 2012), or simple statistical measures of word co-occurrence (e.g., the Dice coefficient,[6] log-likelihood ratio) can also act as a means of computing cross-lingual semantic similarity measure $sim(w^s, w^t)$ in lieu of the cosine similarity between word embeddings. Such word translation tables are then used to induce bilingual lexicons, and can be used to build seed lexicons required for, e.g., mapping-based embedding approaches. Aligning each word in a given source language sentence with the most similar target language word from the target language sentence is exactly the same greedy decoding algorithm that is implemented in IBM Model 1. However, unlike cross-lingual word embedding models or traditional approaches from Section 4.1, standalone word alignment algorithms do not allow to learn the word representations $vec(w)$ explicitly.

The main assumption underpinning IBM Model 1 is also present in the joint objective of models that combine two monolingual objective with a cross-lingual regularization, as discussed later in Section 5.1.3. For instance, in the model of Gouws et al. (2015), the cross-lingual regularization penalizes the Euclidean distance between words in two embedding spaces proportional to their alignment frequency. Instead of running the word alignment algorithm on parallel sentences directly, their model assumes *a uniform alignment model* as done in IBM Model 1. Hermann and Blunsom (2014) make the same assumption in their model: they minimize the ℓ_2-loss between the bag-of-word vectors of parallel sentences, which effectively means that they assume a uniform alignment model.

4.3   REPRESENTATIONS BASED ON LATENT AND EXPLICIT CROSS-LINGUAL CONCEPTS

Going back to the high-level formulation of cross-lingual word similarity provided by Equations (4.1) and (4.2), other shared cross-lingual features $c_i, i = 1, \ldots, N$ can be used in lieu of one-to-one translation pairs from a seed bilingual lexicon (see Section 4.1) to span shared cross-lingual semantic spaces. A popular option in previous work is to induce such *latent* shared cross-lingual features directly from word-aligned, sentence-aligned, or document-aligned bilingual data. This is done by means of bilingual probabilistic topic modeling (Boyd-Graber et al., 2017, Vulić et al., 2015). In bilingual probabilistic topic modeling, the goal is to extract a set

---

[2]https://github.com/moses-smt/mgiza
[3]https://github.com/clab/fast_align
[4]https://github.com/redpony/cdec
[5]https://code.google.com/archive/p/berkeleyaligner/
[6]For instance, Levy et al. (2017) show that a class of cross-lingual word embedding algorithms which rely on sentence-aligned data can be seen as a generalization of the Dice Coefficient, commonly used as a baseline in unsupervised word alignment.

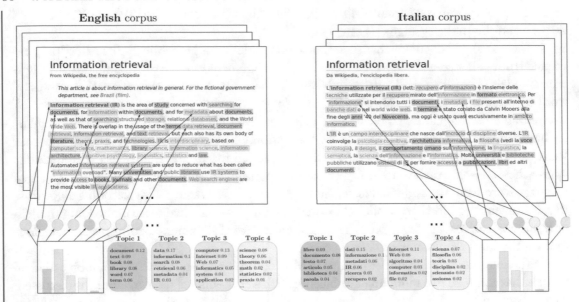

Figure 4.6: An overview of the key intuitions behind bilingual latent topic modeling. Documents are represented as probability distributions over the set of N latent cross-lingual topics induced from a bilingual corpus. Each word token in each document is assigned the actual topic which was used to generate the word token at that position based on the induced per-document topic distributions. Each latent cross-lingual topic has its language-specific representation provided as a probability distribution over the entire source language vocabulary V^s as well as over the entire target language vocabulary V^t.

of N latent shared cross-lingual concepts (i.e., cross-lingual topics) $\{z_1, \ldots, z_N\}$ that optimally describe the data at hand. Extracting latent cross-lingual topics actually implies learning two sets of probability distributions. First, per-topic word distributions contain probability scores $P(w^s|z_n)$ and $P(w^t|z_n)$ which are computed for each latent cross-lingual topic z_n and for each $w^s \in V^s$ and for each $w^t \in V^t$. These distributions can be seen as language-specific representations of a language-independent latent cross-lingual concept/topic. Second, per-document topic distributions with probability scores $P(z_n|d)$, where d is a document provided in any of the two languages, are used to represent each document as a mixture of N latent cross-lingual topics. In summary, each language-independent latent cross-lingual topic z_n has some probability to be found in a particular document (modeled by per-document topic distributions), and each such topic has a language-specific representation in each language (modeled by language-specific per-topic word distributions). The main concepts of bilingual latent topic modeling are illustrated in Figure 4.6.

Cross-lingual word representations are then derived directly from the learned per-topic word distributions. The representation of each word is in fact an N-dimensional vector that stores a conditional topic distribution (Griffiths et al., 2007, Vulić et al., 2011). The representation of each word $w^s \in V^s$ is as follows:

$$vec(w^s) = [(P(z_1|w^s), \ldots, (P(z_n|w^s), \ldots, (P(z_N|w^s)]. \tag{4.3}$$

The analogous representations can be derived for each $w^t \in V^t$. The learned semantic space can be interpreted as a vector space with interpretable vectors: each dimension of the vector is a conditional probability score associating the word with a cross-lingual topic. Two words with similar distributions over the induced latent topics are then considered semantically similar. The similarity can be measured as the similarity of probability distributions using, e.g., Kullback-Leibler or Jensen-Shannon divergence, or the Hellinger distance (Vulić et al., 2015).

The learning process supporting the induction of necessary probability distributions is then steered by the data requirements (i.e., the level of bilingual supervision). Some work relies on pseudo-mixed corpora constructed by merging aligned document pairs, and then applies a monolingual topic model such as Latent Semantic Indexing (LSI) (Landauer and Dumais, 1997), a probabilistic version of LSI (Hofmann, 1999), or Latent Dirichlet Allocation (Blei et al., 2003) on top of the merged data (De Smet et al., 2011, Littman et al., 1998).[7] This approach is very similar to pseudo-cross-lingual approaches to cross-lingual word embedding learning discussed in Chapters 5 and 7. More recent topic models learn on the basis of parallel word-level information, enforcing word pairs from seed bilingual lexicons (again!) to obtain similar topic distributions (Boyd-Graber and Blei, 2009, Boyd-Graber and Resnik, 2010, Jagarlamudi and Daumé III, 2010, Zhang et al., 2010). In consequence, this also influences topic distributions of related words not occurring in the dictionary. Another group of models utilizes alignments at the document level (Fukumasu et al., 2012, Heyman et al., 2016, Mimno et al., 2009, Platt et al., 2010, Vulić et al., 2011) to induce shared topical spaces. The very same level of supervision (i.e., document alignments) is used by several cross-lingual word embedding models, surveyed in Chapter 7.

Instead of learning latent cross-lingual concepts/topics, another line of work labels vector dimensions *explicitly*. The main idea is to start from a knowledge resource such as Wikipedia and index words from both languages according to Wikipedia articles in which the word occurs. In other words, each Wikipedia article is treated as an explicit concept for which a definition or a description is provided in more than one language. Assuming that one possesses N Wikipedia article pairs $c_1 = (c_1^s, c_1^t), \ldots, c_n = (c_n^s, c_n^t), \ldots, c_N = (c_N^s, c_N^t)$ in two languages, the representation of each word $w^s \in V^s$ is then:

$$vec(w^s) = [i(w^s, c_1^s), \ldots, (i(w^s, c_n^s), \ldots, i(w^s, c_N^s)]. \tag{4.4}$$

---

[7]Training topic models on word-document co-occurrence data can be seen as a form of dimensionality reduction. Tracing the genealogy of topic models from LSI to LDA reveals their close relationship to the classical vector space models.

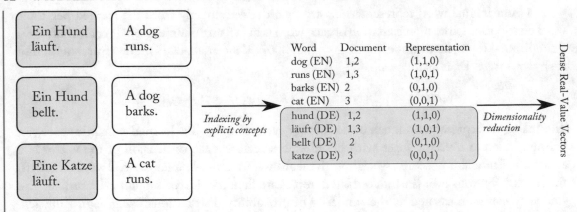

Figure 4.7: Learning cross-lingual word representations based on explicit concepts: indexing based on document or sentence IDs.

Finally, dense word embeddings can be obtained from the high-dimensional word representations based on explicit concept indexing by applying any dimensionality reduction technique (e.g., SVD, PCA). The idea is illustrated in Figure 4.7.

4.4   SUMMARY

All these "historical" architectures measure the strength of cross-lingual word similarities through metrics defined in the cross-lingual space, e.g., Kullback-Leibler or Jensen-Shannon divergence (in topic spaces), or vector inner products (in sparse context-counting vector spaces). Furthermore, they typically learn from the same data and rely on the same bilingual supervision signals as cross-lingual word embedding models. This indicates that cross-lingual architectures are interchangeable within cross-lingual applications and are therefore applicable to NLP tasks that rely on cross-lingual similarity scores. The pre-embedding architectures and more recent cross-lingual word embedding methods have been applied to an overlapping set of evaluation tasks and applications, ranging from bilingual lexicon induction to cross-lingual knowledge transfer, including cross-lingual parser transfer (Ammar et al., 2016a, Täckström et al., 2012), cross-lingual document classification (De Smet et al., 2011, Gabrilovich and Markovitch, 2006, Hermann and Blunsom, 2014, Klementiev et al., 2012), cross-lingual relation extraction (Faruqui and Kumar, 2015), etc. In summary, while sharing the goals and assumptions of older cross-lingual architectures, cross-lingual word embedding methods have capitalized on the recent methodological and algorithmic advances in the field of representation learning, owing their wide use to their simplicity, efficiency and handling of large corpora, as well as their relatively robust performance across domains.

CHAPTER 5

Word-Level Alignment Models

In the following, we will now discuss different types of the current generation of cross-lingual word embedding models, starting with models based on word-level alignment. Among these, as already mentioned, models based on parallel data are more common.

5.1 WORD-LEVEL ALIGNMENT METHODS WITH PARALLEL DATA

We distinguish three methods that use parallel word-aligned data.

(a) **Mapping-based approaches** (also called projection-based approaches) that assume monolingual word representations trained independently on large monolingual corpora and then seek to learn a transformation matrix that maps representations in one language to the representations of the other language. They learn this transformation from word alignments or bilingual dictionaries. As shown in Table 3.1, these approaches are most popular and support cross-lingual word embedding induction in unsupervised and weakly supervised settings.

(b) **Pseudo-mixed approaches** that use monolingual word embedding methods on automatically constructed (or corrupted) corpora that contain words from both the source and the target language. If for any two languages, we had access to huge corpora of humans naturally mixing those languages, as we do for English and Spanish, for example, we could simply apply monolingual word embedding algorithms directly to this data and induce cross-lingual word embeddings. In the absence of such data, some researchers have tried to synthetically create pseudo-mixed language corpora, applying monolingual word embedding algorithms to these.

(c) **Joint methods** that take parallel text as input and minimize the source and target language monolingual losses jointly with a cross-lingual regularization term.

We will show that *modulo* optimization strategies, these approaches are equivalent. Before discussing the first category of methods, we will briefly introduce two concepts that are of relevance in these and the subsequent sections.

Bilingual lexicon induction   Bilingual lexicon induction is the intrinsic task that is most commonly used to evaluate current cross-lingual word embedding models. Briefly, given a list of N

language word forms $w_1^s, \ldots, w_N^s$, the goal is to determine the most appropriate translation w_i^t, for each query form w_i^s. This is commonly accomplished by finding a target language word whose embedding $\mathbf{x}_i^t$ is the nearest neighbor to the source word embedding $\mathbf{x}_i^s$ in the shared semantic space, where similarity is usually computed using a cosine their embeddings. See Chapter 10 for more details.

Hubness   Hubness (Radovanović et al., 2010) is a phenomenon observed in high-dimensional spaces where some points (known as *hubs*) are the nearest neighbors of many other points. As translations are assumed to be nearest neighbors in cross-lingual embedding space, hubness has been reported to affect cross-lingual word embedding models.

5.1.1   MAPPING-BASED APPROACHES

Mapping-based (or projection-based) approaches are by far the most prominent category of cross-lingual word embedding models and—due to their conceptual simplicity and ease of use—are currently the most popular. Mapping-based approaches aim to learn a mapping from the monolingual embedding spaces to a joint cross-lingual space. Approaches in this category differ along multiple dimensions.

1. **The mapping method** that is optimized used to transform the monolingual embedding spaces into a cross-lingual embedding space.

2. **The seed lexicon** that is used to learn the mapping.

3. **The refinement** of the learned mapping.

4. **The retrieval** of the nearest neighbors.

Mapping Methods
Four types of mapping methods have been proposed.

1. **Regression methods** map the embeddings of the source language to the target language space by maximizing their similarity.

2. **Orthogonal methods** map the embeddings in the source language to maximize their similarity with the target language embeddings, but constrain the transformation to be orthogonal.

3. **Canonical methods** map the embeddings of both languages to a new shared space, which maximizes their similarity.

4. **Margin methods** map the embeddings of the source language to maximize the margin between correct translations and other candidates.

Regression methods   One of the most influential methods for learning a mapping is the linear transformation method by Mikolov et al. (2013). The method is motivated by the observation that words and their translations show similar geometric constellations in monolingual embedding spaces after an appropriate linear transformation is applied, as illustrated in Figure 5.1. This suggests that it is possible to transform the vector space of a source language s to the vector space of the target language t by learning a linear projection with a transformation matrix $\mathbf{W}^{s \rightarrow t}$. We use $\mathbf{W}$ in the following if the direction is unambiguous.

Using the $n = 5000$ most frequent words from the source language $w_1^s, \ldots, w_n^s$ and their translations $w_1^t, \ldots, w_n^t$ as seed words, they learn $\mathbf{W}$ using stochastic gradient descent by minimizing the squared Euclidean distance (mean squared error, MSE) between the previously learned monolingual representations of the source seed word $\mathbf{x}_i^s$ that is transformed using $\mathbf{W}$ and its translation $\mathbf{x}_i^t$ in the bilingual dictionary:

$$\Omega_{\text{MSE}} = \sum_{i=1}^{n} \| \mathbf{W}\mathbf{x}_i^s - \mathbf{x}_i^t \|^2. \tag{5.1}$$

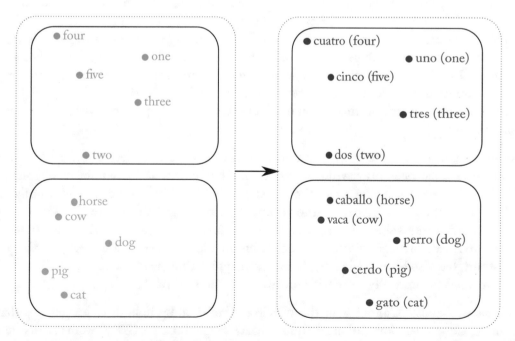

Figure 5.1: Similar geometric relations between numbers and animals in English and Spanish (Mikolov et al., 2013b). Words embeddings are projected to two dimensions using PCA and are manually rotated to emphasize the similarity of constellations in the respective monolingual embedding spaces.

This can also be written in matrix form as minimizing the squared Frobenius norm of the residual matrix:

$$\Omega_{\text{MSE}} = \|\mathbf{W}\mathbf{X}^s - \mathbf{X}^t\|_F^2, \tag{5.2}$$

where $\mathbf{X}^s$ and $\mathbf{X}^t$ are the embedding matrices of the seed words in the source and target language respectively. Analogously, the problem can be seen as finding a least squares solution to a system of linear equations with multiple right-hand sides:

$$\mathbf{W}\mathbf{X}^s = \mathbf{X}^t. \tag{5.3}$$

A common solution to this problem enables calculating $\mathbf{W}$ analytically as $\mathbf{W} = \mathbf{X}^+\mathbf{X}^t$ where $\mathbf{X}^+ = (\mathbf{X}^{s\top}\mathbf{X}^s)^{-1}\mathbf{X}^{s\top}$ is the Moore–Penrose pseudoinverse.

In our notation, the MSE mapping approach can be seen as optimizing the following objective:

$$J = \underbrace{\mathcal{L}_{\text{SGNS}}(\mathbf{X}^s) + \mathcal{L}_{\text{SGNS}}(\mathbf{X}^t)}_{1} + \underbrace{\Omega_{\text{MSE}}(\underline{\mathbf{X}^s}, \underline{\mathbf{X}^t}, \mathbf{W})}_{2}. \tag{5.4}$$

First, each of the monolingual losses is optimized independently. Second, the regularization term Ω_{MSE} is optimized while keeping the induced monolingual embeddings fixed. The basic approach of Mikolov et al. (2013) has later been adopted by many others who for instance incorporated ℓ_2 regularization (Dinu et al., 2015). A common preprocessing step that is applied to the monolingual embeddings is to normalize the monolingual embeddings to be unit length. Xing et al. (2015) argue that this normalization resolves an inconsistency between the metric used for training (dot product) and the metric used for evaluation (cosine similarity).[1] Artetxe et al. (2016) motivate length normalization to ensure that all training instances contribute equally to the objective.

Orthogonal methods   The most common way in which the basic regression method of the previous section has been improved is to constrain the transformation $\mathbf{W}$ to be orthogonal, i.e., $\mathbf{W}^\top\mathbf{W} = \mathbf{I}$. The exact solution under this constraint is $\mathbf{W} = \mathbf{V}\mathbf{U}^\top$ and can be efficiently computed in linear time with respect to the vocabulary size using SVD where $\mathbf{X}^{t\top}\mathbf{X}^s = \mathbf{U}\boldsymbol{\Sigma}\mathbf{V}^\top$. This constraint is motivated by Xing et al. (2015) to preserve length normalization. Artetxe et al. (2016) motivate orthogonality as a means to ensure monolingual invariance. An orthogonality constraint has also been used to regularize the mapping (Zhang et al., 2017a, 2016b) and has been motivated theoretically to be self-consistent (Smith et al., 2017).

Canonical methods   Canonical methods map the embeddings in both languages to a shared space using Canonical Correlation Analysis (CCA). Haghighi et al. (2008) were the first to use this method for learning translation lexicons for the words of different languages. Faruqui and Dyer (2014) later applied CCA to project words from two languages into a shared embedding space. Whereas linear projection only learns one transformation matrix $\mathbf{W}^{s\to t}$ to project the

---

[1] For unit vectors, dot product and cosine similarity are equivalent.

embedding space of a source language into the space of a target language, CCA learns a transformation matrix for the source and target language $\mathbf{W}^{s\rightarrow}$ and $\mathbf{W}^{t\rightarrow}$, respectively, to project them into a new joint space that is different from both the space of s and of t. We can write the correlation between a projected source language embedding vector $\mathbf{W}^{s\rightarrow}\mathbf{x}_i^s$ and its corresponding projected target language embedding vector $\mathbf{W}^{t\rightarrow}\mathbf{x}_i^t$ as:

$$\rho(\mathbf{W}^{s\rightarrow}\mathbf{x}_i^s, \mathbf{W}^{t\rightarrow}\mathbf{x}_i^t) = \frac{\mathrm{cov}(\mathbf{W}^{s\rightarrow}\mathbf{x}_i^s, \mathbf{W}^{t\rightarrow}\mathbf{x}_i^t)}{\sqrt{\mathrm{var}(\mathbf{W}^{s\rightarrow}\mathbf{x}_i^s)\mathrm{var}(\mathbf{W}^{t\rightarrow}\mathbf{x}_i^t)}}, \tag{5.5}$$

where $\mathrm{cov}(\cdot, \cdot)$ is the covariance and $\mathrm{var}(\cdot)$ is the variance. CCA then aims to maximize the correlation (or analogously minimize the negative correlation) between the projected vectors $\mathbf{W}^{s\rightarrow}\mathbf{x}_i^s$ and $\mathbf{W}^{t\rightarrow}\mathbf{x}_i^t$:

$$\Omega_{\mathrm{CCA}} = -\sum_{i=1}^{n} \rho(\mathbf{W}^{s\rightarrow}\mathbf{x}_i^s, \mathbf{W}^{t\rightarrow}\mathbf{x}_i^t). \tag{5.6}$$

We can write their objective in our notation as the following:

$$J = \underbrace{\mathcal{L}_{\mathrm{LSA}}(\mathbf{X}^s) + \mathcal{L}_{\mathrm{LSA}}(\mathbf{X}^t)}_{1} + \underbrace{\Omega_{\mathrm{CCA}}(\underline{\mathbf{X}}^s, \underline{\mathbf{X}}^t, \mathbf{W}^{s\rightarrow}, \mathbf{W}^{t\rightarrow})}_{2}. \tag{5.7}$$

Faruqui and Dyer (2014) propose to use the 80% projection vectors with the highest correlation. Lu et al. (2015) incorporate a nonlinearity into the canonical method by training two deep neural networks to maximize the correlation between the projections of both monolingual embedding spaces. Ammar et al. (2016) extend the canonical approach to multiple languages.

Artetxe et al. (2016) show that the canonical method is similar to the orthogonal method with dimension-wise mean centering. Artetxe et al. (2018) show that regression methods, canonical methods, and orthogonal methods can be seen as instances of a framework that includes optional weighting, mean centering, whitening, and de-whitening steps, which further demonstrates the similarity of existing approaches.

Margin methods Lazaridou et al. (2015) optimize a max-margin based ranking loss instead of MSE to reduce hubness. This max-margin based ranking loss is essentially the same as the MML Collobert and Weston (2008) used for learning monolingual embeddings. Instead of assigning higher scores to correct sentence windows, we now try to assign a higher cosine similarity to word pairs that are translations of each other ($\mathbf{x}_i^s, \mathbf{x}_i^t$; first term below) than random word pairs ($\mathbf{x}_i^s, \mathbf{x}_j^t$; second term):

$$\Omega_{\mathrm{MML}} = \sum_{i=1}^{n} \sum_{j\neq i}^{k} \max\{0, \gamma - \cos(\mathbf{W}\mathbf{x}_i^s, \mathbf{x}_i^t) + \cos(\mathbf{W}\mathbf{x}_i^s, \mathbf{x}_j^t)\}. \tag{5.8}$$

The choice of the k negative examples, which we compare against the translations is crucial. Dinu et al. (2015) propose to select negative examples that are more informative by being near the current projected vector $\mathbf{Wx}_i^s$ but far from the actual translation vector $\mathbf{x}_i^t$. Unlike random intruders, such intelligently chosen intruders help the model identify training instances where the model considerably fails to approximate the target function. In the formulation adopted in this article, their objective becomes:

$$J = \underbrace{\mathcal{L}_{\text{CBOW}}(\mathbf{X}^s) + \mathcal{L}_{\text{CBOW}}(\mathbf{X}^t)}_{1} + \underbrace{\Omega_{\text{MML-I}}(\underline{\mathbf{X}^s}, \underline{\mathbf{X}^t}, \mathbf{W})}_{2}, \tag{5.9}$$

where $\Omega_{\text{MML-I}}$ designates Ω_{MML} with intruders as negative examples.

Among the presented mapping approaches, orthogonal methods are the most commonly adopted as the orthogonality constraint has been shown to improve over the basic regression method.

The Seed Lexicon

The seed lexicon is another core component of any mapping-based approach. In the past, three types of seed lexicons have been used to learn a joint cross-lingual word embedding space:

1. an **off-the-shelf** bilingal lexicon;

2. a **weakly supervised** bilingual lexicon; and

3. a **learned** bilingual lexicon.

Off-the-shelf   Most early approaches (Mikolov et al., 2013b) employed off-the-shelf or automatically generated bilingual lexicons of frequent words. Later approaches reduce the number of seed pairs, demonstrating that it is feasible to learn a cross-lingual word embedding space with as little as 25 seed pairs (Artetxe et al., 2017).

Weak supervision   Other approaches employ weak supervision to create seed lexicons based on cognates (Smith et al., 2017), shared numerals (Artetxe et al., 2017), or identically spelled strings (Søgaard et al., 2018).

Learned   Recently, approaches have been proposed that learn an initial seed lexicon in a completely unsupervised way. We cover these methods in more detail in Chapter 9. Interestingly, so far, all unsupervised cross-lingual word embedding methods are based on the mapping approach. Conneau et al. (2018) learn an initial mapping in an adversarial way by additionally training a discriminator to differentiate between projected and actual target language embeddings. Artetxe et al. (2018) propose to use an initialization method based on the heuristic that translations have similar similarity distributions across languages. Hoshen and Wolf (2018) first project vectors of the N most frequent words to a lower-dimensional space with PCA. They then aim to find a optimal using that minimizes the sum of Euclidean distances by learning $\mathbf{W}^{s \rightarrow t}$ and $\mathbf{W}^{t \rightarrow s}$ and enforce cyclical consistency constraints that force vectors round-projected to the other language space and back to remain unchanged. Alvarez-Melis and Jaakkola (2018) solve an optimal transport in order to learn an alignment between the monolingual word embedding spaces.

The Refinement

Many mapping-based approaches propose to refine the mapping to improve the quality of the initial seed lexicon. Vulić and Korhonen (2016) propose to learn a first shared bilingual embedding space based on an existing cross-lingual embedding model. They retrieve the translations of frequent source words in this cross-lingual embedding space, which they use as seed words to learn a second mapping. To ensure that the retrieved translations are reliable, they propose a symmetry constraint: Translation pairs are only retained if their projected embeddings are mutual nearest neighbors in the cross-lingual embedding space. This constraint is meant to reduce hubness and has been adopted later in many subsequent unsupervised methods that rely on refinement (Artetxe et al., 2018b, Conneau et al., 2018). See Chapter 9.

Rather than just performing one step of refinement, Artetxe et al. (2017) propose a method that iteratively learns a new mapping by using translation pairs from the previous mapping. Training is terminated when the improvement on the average dot product for the induced dictionary falls below a given threshold from one iteration to the next. Ruder et al. (2018) solve a sparse linear assignment problem in order to refine the mapping. As discussed in Chapter 4, the refinement idea is conceptually similar to the work of Peirsman and Padó (2010, 2011) and Vulić and Moens (2013), with the difference that earlier approaches were developed within the traditional cross-lingual distributional framework (mapping vectors into the count-based space using a seed lexicon). Glavaš et al. (2019) propose to learn a matrix $\mathbf{W}^{s \rightarrow t}$ and a matrix $\mathbf{W}^{t \rightarrow s}$. They then use the intersection of the translation pairs obtained from both mappings in the subsequent iteration. While refinement is less crucial when a large seed lexicon is available, approaches that learn a mapping from a small seed lexicon or in a completely unsupervised way often rely on refinement (Artetxe et al., 2018b, Conneau et al., 2018).

The Retrieval

Most existing methods retrieve translations as the nearest neighbors of the source word embeddings in the cross-lingual embedding space based on cosine similarity. Dinu et al. (2015) propose to use a globally corrected neighbor retrieval method instead to reduce hubness. Smith et al. (2017) propose a similar solution to the hubness issue: they invert the softmax used for finding the translation of a word at test time and normalize the probability over source words rather than target words. Conneau et al. (2018) propose an alternative similarity measure called cross-domain similarity local scaling (CSLS), which is defined as:

$$\text{CSLS}(\mathbf{W}\mathbf{x}^s, \mathbf{x}^t) = 2\cos(\mathbf{W}\mathbf{x}^s, \mathbf{x}^t) - r^t(\mathbf{W}\mathbf{x}^s) - r^s(\mathbf{x}^t), \tag{5.10}$$

where r^t is the mean similarity of a target word to its neighborhood, defined as $r^t(\mathbf{W}\mathbf{x}_s) = \frac{1}{K} \sum_{\mathbf{x}_t \in \mathcal{N}^t(\mathbf{W}\mathbf{x}^s)} \cos(\mathbf{W}\mathbf{x}^s, \mathbf{x}^t)$ where $\mathcal{N}^t(\mathbf{W}\mathbf{x}^s)$ is the neighborhood of the projected source word. Intuitively, CSLS increases the similarity of isolated word vectors and decreases the similarity of hubs. CSLS has been shown to significantly increase the accuracy of bilingual lexicon induction and is nowadays mostly used in lieu of cosine similarity for nearest neighbor retrieval. Joulin et al.

(2018) propose to optimize this metric directly when learning the mapping. Retrieval methods are discussed again in Chapter 9, since retrieval heuristics have proven particularly important in the context of unsupervised methods.

Cross-lingual embeddings via retrofitting   Learning a mapping between unaligned monolingual embedding spaces using word-level supervision (from dictionaries or multilingual knowledge bases such as BabelNet) can also be framed as a retrofitting problem (Faruqui et al., 2015). The idea is to inject knowledge from semantic lexicons into pre-trained distributional (i.e., corpus-based) word embeddings. Retrofitting tries to create a new word embedding matrix $\hat{\mathbf{X}}$ whose embeddings $\hat{\mathbf{x}}_i$ are both close to the corresponding learned monolingual word embeddings $\mathbf{x}_i$ as well as close to their neighbors $\hat{\mathbf{x}}_j$ in a knowledge graph:

$$\Omega_{\text{retro}} = \sum_{i=1}^{|V|} \left[\alpha_i \| \hat{\mathbf{x}}_i - \mathbf{x}_i \|^2 + \sum_{(i,j) \in E} \beta_{ij} \| \hat{\mathbf{x}}_i - \hat{\mathbf{x}}_j \|^2 \right], \tag{5.11}$$

where E is the set of edges in the knowledge graph and α and β control the strength of the contribution of each term.

In contrast to previous work, retrofitting approaches use constraints on each word rather than a translation matrix $\mathbf{W}$ to arrive at a new cross-lingual vector space. While these constraints can capture relations that are more complex than a linear transformation, the original post-processing retrofitting approaches are limited to words that are contained in the semantic lexicons, and do not generalize to words unobserved in the external semantic databases. In other words, the goal of retrofitting methods is to refine vectors of words for which additional high-quality lexical information exists in the external resource, while the methods still back off to distributional vector estimates for all other words.

While the initial retrofitting work focused solely on monolingual word embeddings (Faruqui et al., 2015, Wieting et al., 2015), Mrkšić et al. (2017) derive both monolingual and cross-lingual synonymy *and* antonymy constraints from BabelNet. They then use these constraints to bring the monolingual vector spaces of two different languages together into a shared embedding space. Such retrofitting approaches employ Ω_{MMHL} with a careful selection of intruders, similar to the work of Lazaridou et al. (2015). In contrast to previous work, retrofitting approaches use constraints on each word rather than a translation matrix $\mathbf{W}$ to arrive at a new cross-lingual vector space. While these constraints can capture relations that are more complex than a linear transformation, as mentioned previously, they are limited to words that are contained in the semantic lexicons.

To remedy the issue with words unobserved in the external resources and learn a global transformation of the entire distributional space in both languages, several methods have been proposed. Post-specialization approaches first fine-tune vectors of words observed in the external resources, and then aim to learn a global transformation function using the original distributional vectors and their retrofitted counterparts as training pairs. The transformation function can be implemented as a deep feed-forward neural network with nonlinear transformations (Vulić et al., 2018), or it can be enriched by an adversarial component that tries to distinguish between distributional and retrofitted vectors (Ponti et al., 2018). While this is a two-step process—(1.) retrofitting and (2.) global transformation learning—an alternative approach proposed by Glavaš and Vulić (2018) learns a global transformation function directly in one step using external lexical knowledge. Furthermore, Pandey et al. (2017) explored the orthogonal idea of using cross-lingual word embeddings to transfer the regularization effect of knowledge bases using retrofitting techniques.

5.1.2   PSEUDO-MIXING APPROACHES

Rather than learning a mapping between the source and the target language, some approaches use the word-level alignment of a seed bilingual dictionary to construct a pseudo-bilingual mixed language corpus by randomly replacing words in a source language corpus with their translations. Xiao and Guo (2014) propose the first such method. They first construct a seed bilingual dictionary by translating all words that appear in the source language corpus into the target language using Wiktionary, filtering polysemous words as well as translations that do not appear in the target language corpus. From this seed dictionary, they create a joint vocabulary, in which each translation pair occupies the same vector representation. They train this model using MMHL (Collobert and Weston, 2008) by feeding it context windows of both the source and target language corpus.

Other approaches explicitly create a pseudo-mixed language corpus: Gouws and Søgaard (2015) concatenate the source and target language corpus and replace each word that is part of a translation pair with its translation equivalent with a probability of $\frac{1}{2k_t}$, where k_t is the total number of possible translation equivalents for a word, and train CBOW on this corpus. See Wick et al. (2016) for a very similar follow-up. Ammar et al. (2016b) extend this approach to multiple languages: using bilingual dictionaries, they determine clusters of synonymous words in different languages. They then concatenate the monolingual corpora of different languages and replace tokens in the same cluster with the cluster ID. Finally, they train SGNS on the concatenated corpus.

Duong et al. (2016) propose a similar approach. Instead of randomly replacing every word in the corpus with its translation, they replace each center word with a translation on-the-fly during CBOW training. In addition, they handle polysemy explicitly by proposing an EM-inspired method that chooses as replacement the translation w_i^t whose representation is most similar to the sum of the source word representation $\mathbf{x}_i^s$ and the sum of the context embeddings $\mathbf{x}_s^s$ as in Equation (2.9):

$$w_i^t = \operatorname{argmax}_{w' \in \tau(w_i)} \cos(\mathbf{x}_i + \mathbf{x}_s^s, \mathbf{x}'). \tag{5.12}$$

They jointly learn to predict both the words and their appropriate translations using PanLex as the seed bilingual dictionary. PanLex covers around 1,300 language with about 12 million expressions. Consequently, translations are high coverage but often noisy. Adams et al. (2017) use the same approach for pre-training cross-lingual word embeddings for low-resource language modeling. Section 5.1.4 shows that these pseudo-mixing models are in fact optimizing for the same objective as the mapping models discussed earlier (Mikolov et al., 2013b).

5.1.3 JOINT APPROACHES

While the previous approaches either optimize a set of monolingual losses and then the cross-lingual regularization term (mapping-based approaches) or optimize a monolingual loss and implicitly—via data manipulation—a cross-lingual regularization term, joint approaches optimize monolingual and cross-lingual objectives in parallel.

Klementiev et al. (2012) cast learning cross-lingual representations as a multi-task learning problem. They jointly optimize a source language and target language model together with a cross-lingual regularization term that encourages words that are often aligned with each other in a parallel corpus to be similar. The monolingual objective is the classical LM objective of minimizing the negative log likelihood of the current word w_i given its C previous context words (Bengio et al., 2003):

$$\mathcal{L} = -\log P(w_i \mid w_{i-C+1:i-1}).$$ (5.13)

For the cross-lingual regularization term, they first obtain an alignment matrix $\mathbf{A}^{s \to t}$ (from GIZA++ or similar) that indicates how often each source language word was aligned with each target language word from parallel data such as the Europarl corpus (Koehn, 2009). The cross-lingual regularization term then encourages the representations of source and target language words that are often aligned in $\mathbf{A}^{s \to t}$ to be similar:

$$\Omega_s = -\sum_{i=1}^{|V|^s} \frac{1}{2} \mathbf{x}_i^{s\top} (\mathbf{A}^{s \to t} \otimes \mathbf{I}) \mathbf{x}_i^s,$$ (5.14)

where $\mathbf{I}$ is the identity matrix and $\otimes$ is the Kronecker product. The final regularization term will be the sum of Ω_s and the analogous term for the other direction (Ω_t). Note that Equation (5.14) is a weighted (by word alignment scores) average of inner products and, hence, for unit length normalized embeddings, equivalent to approaches that maximize the sum of the cosine similarities of aligned word pairs. Using $\mathbf{A}^{s \to t} \otimes \mathbf{I}$ to encode interaction is borrowed from linear multi-task learning models (Cavallanti et al., 2010). There, an interaction matrix $\mathbf{A}$ encodes the relatedness between tasks. The complete objective is the following:

$$J = \mathcal{L}(\mathbf{X}_s) + \mathcal{L}(\mathbf{X}_t) + \Omega(\underline{\mathbf{A}^{s \to t}}, \mathbf{X}_s) + \Omega(\underline{\mathbf{A}^{t \to s}}, \mathbf{X}_t).$$ (5.15)

Shi et al. (2015) propose a similar model, but instead of using the objective proposed by Bengio et al. (2003), they use $\mathcal{L}_{\text{GloVe}}$ as their monolingual loss function (see Chapter 2). For cross-lingual regularization, they use a Ω_{MSE} term penalizing the sum of the inner product of alignment probabilities (from GIZA++ or similar) and the Euclidean distances in the cross-lingual space.

Vyas and Carpuat (2016) propose another method based on matrix factorization that enables learning sparse cross-lingual word embeddings. As the sparse cross-lingual word embeddings are different from the monolingual word embeddings $\mathbf{X}$, we diverge slightly from our notation and designate them as $\mathbf{S}$. They propose two constraints: the first constraint induces monolingual sparse representations from pre-trained monolingual word embedding matrices $\mathbf{X}^s$ and $\mathbf{X}^t$ by factorizing each embedding matrix $\mathbf{X}$ into two matrices $\mathbf{S}$ and $\mathbf{E}$ with an additional ℓ_1 constraint on $\mathbf{S}$ for sparsity:

$$\mathcal{L} = \sum_{i=1}^{|V|} \|\mathbf{S}_i \mathbf{E}^\top - \mathbf{X}_i\|_2^2 + \lambda \|\mathbf{S}_i\|_1. \tag{5.16}$$

To learn bilingual word embeddings, they add the second constraint based on the alignment matrix $\mathbf{A}^{s\rightarrow t}$ (from GIZA++) that minimizes the ℓ_2 reconstruction error between words that were strongly aligned to each other in a parallel corpus:

$$\Omega = \sum_{i=1}^{|V^s|} \sum_{j=1}^{|V^t|} \frac{1}{2} \lambda_x \mathbf{A}_{ij}^{s\rightarrow t} \|\mathbf{S}_i^s - \mathbf{S}_j^t\|_2^2. \tag{5.17}$$

The complete optimization then consists of first pre-training monolingual word embeddings $\mathbf{X}^s$ and $\mathbf{X}^t$ with GloVe and in a second step factorizing the monolingual word embeddings with the cross-lingual constraint to induce cross-lingual sparse representations $\mathbf{S}^s$ and $\mathbf{S}^t$:

$$J = \underbrace{\mathcal{L}_{\text{GloVe}}(\mathbf{X}^s) + \mathcal{L}_{\text{GloVe}}(\mathbf{X}^t)}_{1} + \underbrace{\mathcal{L}(\underline{\mathbf{X}^s}, \mathbf{S}^s, \mathbf{E}^s) + \mathcal{L}(\underline{\mathbf{X}^t}, \mathbf{S}^t, \mathbf{E}^t) + \Omega(\mathbf{A}^{s\rightarrow t}, \mathbf{S}^s, \mathbf{S}^t)}_{2}. \tag{5.18}$$

Guo et al. (2015) similarly create target a target language word embedding $\mathbf{x}_i^t$ of a source word w_i^s by taking the average of the embeddings of its translations $\tau(w_i^s)$ weighted by their alignment probability (from, say, GIZA++) with the source word:

$$\mathbf{x}_i^t = \sum_{w_j^t \in \tau(w_i^s)} \frac{\mathbf{A}_{i,j}}{\mathbf{A}_{i,\cdot}} \cdot \mathbf{x}_j^t. \tag{5.19}$$

They propagate alignments to out-of-vocabulary (OOV) words using edit distance as an approximation for morphological similarity and set the target word embedding $\mathbf{x}_k^t$ of an OOV source word w_k^s as the average of the projected vectors of source words that are similar to it based on the edit distance measure:

$$\mathbf{x}_k^t = \frac{1}{|E_k|} \sum_{w^s \in E_k} \mathbf{x}^t, \tag{5.20}$$

where $\mathbf{x}^t$ is the target language word embedding of a source word w^s as created above, $E_k = \{w^s \mid EditDist(w_k^s, w^s) \le \chi\}$, and χ is set empirically to 1.

5.1.4   SOMETIMES MAPPING, JOINT, AND PSEUDO-BILINGUAL APPROACHES ARE EQUIVALENT

In this section we show that while mapping, joint, and pseudo-bilingual approaches seem very different, intuitively, they can sometimes be very similar, and in fact, equivalent. We prove this by first defining a pseudo-bilingual approach that is equivalent to an established joint learning technique; and by then showing that same joint learning technique is equivalent to a popular mapping-based approach (for a particular hyper-parameter setting).

We define CONSTRAINED BILINGUAL SGNS. First, recall that in the negative sampling objective of SGNS in Equation (2.7), the probability of observing a word w with a context word c with representations $\mathbf{x}$ and $\tilde{\mathbf{x}}$ respectively is given as $P(c \mid w) = \sigma(\tilde{\mathbf{x}}^\top \mathbf{x})$, where σ denotes the sigmoid function. We now sample a set of k negative examples, that is, contexts c_i with which w does not occur, as well as actual contexts C consisting of (w_j, c_j) pairs, and try to maximize the above for actual contexts and minimize it for negative samples. Second, recall that Mikolov et al. (2013) obtain cross-lingual embeddings by running SGNS over two monolingual corpora of two different languages at the same time with the constraint that words known to be translation equivalents, according to some dictionary D, have the same representation. We will refer to this as CONSTRAINED BILINGUAL SGNS. This is also the approach taken in Xiao and Guo (2014). D is a function from words w into their translation equivalents w' with the representation $\mathbf{x}'$. With some abuse of notation, we can write the CONSTRAINED BILINGUAL SGNS objective for the source language (idem for the target language):

$$\sum_{(w_j, c_j) \in C} \log \sigma \left(\tilde{\mathbf{x}}_j^\top \mathbf{x}_j \right) + \sum_{i=1}^{k} \log \sigma \left(-\tilde{\mathbf{x}}_i^\top \mathbf{x}_j \right) + \Omega_\infty \sum_{w' \in \tau(w_j)} \left| \mathbf{x}_j - \mathbf{x}_j' \right|. \tag{5.21}$$

In pseudo-bilingual approaches, we instead sample sentences from the corpora in the two languages. When we encounter a word w for which we have a translation, that is, $\tau(w) \neq \emptyset$ we flip a coin and if heads, we replace w with a randomly selected member of $D(w)$. In the case, where D is bijective as in the work of Xiao and Guo (2014), it is easy to see that the two approaches are equivalent, in the limit: sampling mixed $\langle w, c \rangle$-pairs, w and $D(w)$ will converge to the same representations. We can loosen the requirement that D is bijective. To see this, assume, for example, the following word-context pairs: $\langle a, b \rangle, \langle a, c \rangle, \langle a, d \rangle$. The vocabulary of our source language is $\{a, b, d\}$, and the vocabulary of our target language is $\{a, c, d\}$. Let a_s denote the source language word in the word pair a; etc. To obtain a mixed corpus, such that running SGNS directly on it, will induce the same representations, in the limit, simply enumerate all combinations: $\langle a_s, b \rangle, \langle a_t, b \rangle, \langle a_s, c \rangle, \langle a_t, c \rangle, \langle a_s, d_s \rangle, \langle a_s, d_t \rangle, \langle a_t, d_s \rangle, \langle a_t, d_t \rangle$. Note that this is exactly the mixed corpus you would obtain in the limit with the approach by Gouws and Søgaard (2015). Since this reduction generalizes to all examples where D is bijective, this translation provides a constructive proof that for any CONSTRAINED BILINGUAL SGNS model, there exists a corpus such that pseudo-bilingual sampling learns the same embeddings as this model. In order to complete the proof, we need to establish equivalence in the other direction: since the mixed corpus constructed using the method in Gouws and Søgaard (2015) samples from all replacements licensed by the dictionary, in the limit all words in the dictionary are distributionally similar and will, in the limit, be represented by the same vector representation. This is exactly Constrained Bilingual SGNS. Thus, we have the following lemma.

Lemma 5.1   *Pseudo-bilingual sampling is, in the limit, equivalent to* Constrained Bilingual SGNS.

While mapping-based and joint approaches seem very different at first sight, they can also be very similar—and, in fact, sometimes equivalent. We give an example of this by proving two methods in the literature are equivalent under some hyper-parameter settings:

Consider the mapping approach in Faruqui et al. (2015) (*retrofitting*) and Constrained Bilingual SGNS (Xiao and Guo, 2014). Retrofitting requires two pretrained monolingual embeddings. Let us assume these embeddings were induced using SGNS with a set of hyper-parameters $\mathcal{Y}$. Retrofitting minimizes the weighted sum of the Euclidean distances between the seed words and their translation equivalents and their neighbors in the monolingual embeddings, with a parameter α that controls the strength of the regularizer. As this parameter goes to infinity, translation equivalents will be forced to have the same representation. As is the case in Constrained Bilingual SGNS, all word pairs in the seed dictionary will be associated with the same vector representation.

Since retrofitting only affects words in the seed dictionary, the representation of the words not seen in the seed dictionary is determined entirely by the monolingual objectives. Again, this is the same as in Constrained Bilingual SGNS. In other words, if we fix $\mathcal{Y}$ for retrofitting and Constrained Bilingual SGNS, and set the regularization strength $\alpha = \Omega_\infty$ in retrofitting, retrofitting is equivalent to Constrained Bilingual SGNS.

Lemma 5.2   *Retrofitting of SGNS vector spaces with* $\alpha = \Omega_\infty$ *is equivalent to* Constrained Bilingual SGNS.[2]

Proof. We provide a simple bidirectional constructive proof, defining a translation function τ from each retrofitting model $r_i = \langle S, T, (S, T)/\sim, \alpha = \Omega_\infty \rangle$, with S and T source and target SGNS embeddings, and $(S, T)/\sim$ an equivalence relation between source and target embeddings $(w, \mathbf{w})$, with $\mathbf{w} \in \mathbb{R}^d$, to a Constrained Bilingual SGNS model $c_i = \langle S, T, D \rangle$, and back.

Retrofitting minimizes the weighted sum of the Euclidean distances between the seed words and their translation equivalents and their neighbors in the monolingual embeddings, with a parameter α that controls the strength of the regularizer. As this parameter goes to infinity ($\alpha \longmapsto \Omega_\infty$), translation equivalents will be forced to have the same representation. In both

---

[2]All other hyper-parameters are shared and equal, including the dimensionality d of the vector spaces.

retrofitting and CONSTRAINED BILINGUAL SGNS, only words in $(S, T)/ \sim$ and D are directly affected by regularization; the other words only indirectly by being penalized for not being close to distributionally similar words in $(S, T)/ \sim$ and D.

We therefore define $\tau(\langle S, T, (S, T)/ \sim, \alpha = \Omega_\infty \rangle) = \langle S, T, D \rangle$, s.t., $(s, t) \in D$ if and only if $(s, t) \in (S, T)/ \sim$. Since this function is bijective, τ^{-1} provides the backward function from CONSTRAINED BILINGUAL SGNS models to retrofitting models. This completes the proof that retrofitting of SGNS vector spaces and CONSTRAINED BILINGUAL SGNS are equivalent when $\alpha = \Omega_\infty$.

$\square$

○ **Open Problem**   Is there a translation from retrofitting with any α into a pseudo-mixed approach with non-uniform replacement probabilities? The intuition behind this would be that by sampling dictionary replacements less often would correspond to less retrofitting, i.e., using α to down-weigh the cross-lingual consistency.

5.2   WORD-LEVEL ALIGNMENT METHODS WITH COMPARABLE DATA

All previous methods required word-level *parallel* data. We categorize methods that employ word-level alignment with *comparable* data into two types.

(a) Approaches based on **language grounding** correlate the occurrence of words with extra-linguistic features such as images or gaze (eye-tracking data) and use these features to measure the similarity of words across languages.

(b) Approaches based on **comparable features** across languages. The main examples of such features are parts of speech and ortographic features.

Language grounding   Several papers have explored the idea of grounding the semantics of words in a language-independent way by seeing how words co-occur with images or image features. Bicycles always look like bicycles—independently of whether they are called *fiets*, *Fahrrad*, *bicikl*, *bicicletta*, or *vélo*—and since bikes can be automatically detected, computer vision models can represent the generics of bikes. If we associate all these words with such representations, we have a perfect cross-lingual word embedding space.

Bergsma and Van Durme (2011) calculate a similarity score for a pair of words based on the visual similarity of their associated image sets. They propose two strategies to calculate the cosine similarity between the color and SIFT features (Lowe, 2004) of two image sets. They either take the average of the maximum similarity scores (AVGMAX) or the maximum of the maximum similarity scores (MAXMAX). Kiela et al. (2015) propose doing the same but use CNN-based image features. Vulić et al. (2016) in addition propose to combine image and word representations either by interpolating and concatenating them or by interpolating the linguistic and visual similarity scores.

A similar idea of grounding language for learning multimodal multilingual representations can be applied for sensory signals beyond vision, e.g., auditive or olfactory signals (Kiela and Clark, 2015). This line of work, however, is currently under-explored. Moreover, it seems that signals from other modalities are typically more useful as an additional source of information to complement the uni-modal signals from text, rather than using other modalities as the single source of information.

One alternative way of embedding words by grounding them in extra-linguistic context uses features that reflect human cognitive processing. Barrett et al. (2016) show that gaze features (measures obtained from eye-tracking recordings) in some cases transfer across languages, and Søgaard (2016) speculate whether fMRI signals would do so, too.

Comparable features   Other approaches rely on comparability between certain features of a word, such as its part-of-speech tag. Gouws and Søgaard (2015) create a pseudo-mixed language corpus by replacing words based on part-of-speech equivalence, that is, words with the same part-of-speech in different languages are replaced with one another. Instead of using the POS tags of the source and target words as a bridge between two languages, we can also use the POS tags of their contexts. This makes strong assumptions about the word orders in the two languages, and their similarity, but Duong et al. (2015) use this to obtain cross-lingual word embeddings for several language pairs. They use POS tags as context features and run SGNS on the concatenation of two monolingual corpora. Note that under the (too simplistic) assumptions that all instances of a part-of-speech have the same distribution, and each word belongs to a single part-of-speech class, this approach is equivalent to the pseudo-mixed corpus approach described before.

CHAPTER 6

Sentence-Level Alignment Methods

6.1 SENTENCE-LEVEL METHODS WITH PARALLEL DATA

Large volumes of sentence-aligned parallel data are available for many European languages, which has led to much work focusing on learning cross-lingual representations from sentence-aligned parallel data. For low-resource languages or new domains, sentence-aligned parallel data is hard to get by.

Methods leveraging sentence-aligned data are generally extensions of successful monolingual models. We have detected three main types.

(a) **Compositional sentence models** use word representations to construct sentence representations of aligned sentences, which are trained to be close to each other.

(b) **Bilingual autoencoders** reconstruct source and target sentences using an autoencoder.

(c) **Bilingual skip-gram models** use the skip-gram objective to predict words in both source and target sentences.

Compositional sentence models Hermann and Blunsom (2013) train a model to bring the sentence representations of aligned sentences $sent^s$ and $sent^t$ in source and target language s and t, respectively, close to each other. The representation $\mathbf{y}^s$ of sentence $sent^s$ in language s is the sum of the embeddings of its words:

$$\mathbf{y}^s = \sum_{i=1}^{|sent^s|} \mathbf{x}_i^s. \tag{6.1}$$

They seek to minimize the distance between aligned sentences $sent^s$ and $sent^t$:

$$E_{dist}(sent^s, sent^t) = \|\mathbf{y}^s - \mathbf{y}^t\|^2. \tag{6.2}$$

They optimize this distance using Ω_{MMHL} by learning to bring aligned sentences closer together than randomly sampled negative examples:

$$\Omega_{\text{MMHL}} = \sum_{(sent^s, sent^t) \in C} \sum_{i=1}^{k} \max(0, 1 + E_{dist}(sent^s, sent^t) - E_{dist}(sent^s, s_i^t)), \tag{6.3}$$

where k is the number of negative examples. In addition, they use an ℓ_2 regularization term for each language $\Omega = \dfrac{\lambda}{2}\|\mathbf{X}\|^2$ so that the final loss they optimize is the following:

$$J = \mathcal{L}(\mathbf{X}^s) + \mathcal{L}(\mathbf{X}^t) + \Omega_{\mathrm{MMHL}}(\mathbf{X}^s, \mathbf{X}^t, \mathcal{C}). \tag{6.4}$$

Note that compared to most previous approaches, there is no dedicated monolingual objective and all loss terms are optimized jointly. Note that in this case, the ℓ_2 norm is applied to representations $\mathbf{X}$, which are computed as the difference of sentence representations.

This regularization term *approximates* minimizing the mean squared error between the pair-wise interacting source and target words in a way similar to Gouws et al. (2015). To see this, note that we minimize the squared error between source and target representations, i.e., Ω_{MSE}—this time only not with regard to word embeddings but with regard to sentence representations. As we saw, these sentence representations are just the sum of their constituent word embeddings. In the limit of infinite data, we therefore implicitly optimize Ω_{MSE} over word representations.

Hermann and Blunsom (2014) extend this approach to documents by applying the composition and objective function recursively to compose sentences into documents. They additionally propose a nonlinear composition function based on bigram pairs, which outperforms simple addition on large training datasets, but underperforms it on smaller data:

$$\mathbf{y} = \sum_{i=1}^{n} \tanh(\mathbf{x}_{i-1} + \mathbf{x}_i). \tag{6.5}$$

Soyer et al. (2015) augment this model with a monolingual objective that operates on the phrase level. The objective uses MMHL and is based on the assumption that phrases are typically more similar to their sub-phrases than to randomly sampled phrases:

$$\mathcal{L} = \big[\max(0, m + \|\mathbf{a}_o - \mathbf{a}_i\|^2 - \|\mathbf{a}_o - \mathbf{b}_n\|^2) + \|\mathbf{a}_o - \mathbf{a}_i\|^2\big]\frac{n_i}{n_o}, \tag{6.6}$$

where m is a margin, $\mathbf{a}_o$ is a phrase of length n_o sampled from a sentence, $\mathbf{a}_i$ is a sub-phrase of $\mathbf{a}_o$ of length n_i, and $\mathbf{b}_n$ is a phrase sampled from a random sentence. The additional loss terms are meant to reduce the influence of the margin as a hyperparameter and to compensate for the differences in phrase and sub-phrase length.

Bilingual autoencoders Instead of minimizing the distance between two sentence representations in different languages, Lauly et al. (2013) aim to reconstruct the target sentence from the original source sentence. Analogously to Hermann and Blunsom (2013), they also encode a sentence as the sum of its word embeddings. They then train an auto-encoder with language-specific encoder and decoder layers and hierarchical softmax to reconstruct from each sentence the sentence itself and its translation. In this case, the encoder parameters are the word embedding matrices $\mathbf{X}^s$ and $\mathbf{X}^t$, while the decoder parameters are transformation matrices that project

Table 6.1: A comparison of similarities and differences of the three bilingual skip-gram variants

Model	Alignment Model	Monolingual Losses	Cross-Lingual Regularizer
BilBOWA (Gouws et al., 2015)	Uniform	$\mathcal{L}_{\mathrm{SGNS}}^{s} + \mathcal{L}_{\mathrm{SGNS}}^{t}$	$\Omega_{\mathrm{BILBOWA}}$
Trans-gram (Coulmance et al., 2015)	Uniform	$\mathcal{L}_{\mathrm{SGNS}}^{s} + \mathcal{L}_{\mathrm{SGNS}}^{t}$	$\Omega_{\mathrm{SGNS}}^{s \to t} + \Omega_{\mathrm{SGNS}}^{t \to s}$
BiSkip (Luong et al., 2015)	Monotonic	$\mathcal{L}_{\mathrm{SGNS}}^{s} + \mathcal{L}_{\mathrm{SGNS}}^{t}$	$\Omega_{\mathrm{SGNS}}^{s \to t} + \Omega_{\mathrm{SGNS}}^{t \to s}$

the encoded representation to the output language space. The loss they optimize can be written as follows:

$$J = \mathcal{L}_{\mathrm{AUTO}}^{s \to s} + \mathcal{L}_{\mathrm{AUTO}}^{t \to t} + \mathcal{L}_{\mathrm{AUTO}}^{s \to t} + \mathcal{L}_{\mathrm{AUTO}}^{t \to s}, \tag{6.7}$$

where $\mathcal{L}_{\mathrm{AUTO}}^{s \to t}$ denotes the loss for reconstructing from a sentence in language s to a sentence in language t. Aligned sentences are sampled from parallel text and all losses are optimized jointly.

Chandar et al. (2014) use a binary BOW instead of the hierarchical softmax. To address the increase in complexity due to the higher dimensionality of the BOW, they propose to merge the bags-of-words in a mini-batch into a single BOW and to perform updates based on this merged bag-of-words. They also add a term to the objective function that encourages correlation between the source and target sentence representations by summing the scalar correlations between all dimensions of the two vectors.

Bilingual skip-gram Several authors propose extensions of the monolingual skip-gram with negative sampling (SGNS) model to learn cross-lingual word embeddings. We show their similarities and differences in Table 6.1. All of these models jointly optimize monolingual SGNS losses for each language together with one more cross-lingual regularization terms:

$$J = \mathcal{L}_{\mathrm{SGNS}}^{s} + \mathcal{L}_{\mathrm{SGNS}}^{t} + \Omega \left(\mathbf{X}^{s}, \mathbf{X}^{t}, \mathcal{C} \right). \tag{6.8}$$

Another commonality is that these models do not require word alignments of aligned sentences. Instead, they make different assumptions about the alignment of the data.

Bilingual Bag-of-Words without Word Alignments (BilBOWA) (Gouws et al., 2015) assumes each word in a source sentence is aligned with *every* word in the target sentence. If we knew the word alignments, we would try to bring the embeddings of aligned words in source and target sentences close together. Instead, under a uniform alignment model which perfectly matches the intuition behind the simplest (lexical) word alignment IBM Model 1 (Brown et al., 1993), we try to bring the *average* alignment close together. In other words, we use the means of the word embeddings in a sentence as the sentence representations $\mathbf{y}$ and seek to minimize the distance between aligned sentence representations:

$$\mathbf{y}^s = \frac{1}{|sent^s|} \sum_{i=1}^{|sent^s|} \mathbf{x}_i^s \tag{6.9}$$

$$\Omega_{\text{BILBOWA}} = \sum_{(sent^s, sent^t) \in C} \|\mathbf{y}^s - \mathbf{y}^t\|^2. \tag{6.10}$$

Note that this regularization term is very similar to the objective used in the compositional sentence model (Hermann and Blunsom, 2013) (Equations (6.1) and (6.2)); the only difference is that we use the mean rather than the sum of word embeddings as sentence representations.

Trans-gram (Coulmance et al., 2015) also assumes uniform alignment but uses the SGNS objective as cross-lingual regularization term. Recall that skip-gram with negative sampling seeks to train a model to distinguish context words from negative samples drawn from a noise distribution based on a center word. In the cross-lingual case, we aim to predict words in the aligned target language sentence based on words in the source sentence. Under uniform alignment, we aim to predict *all* words in the target sentence based on each word in the source sentence:

$$\Omega_{\text{SGNS}}^{s \to t} = - \sum_{(sent^s, sent^t) \in C} \frac{1}{|sent^s|} \sum_{t=1}^{|sent^s|} \sum_{j=1}^{|sent^t|} \log P(w_{t+j} \mid w_t), \tag{6.11}$$

where $P(w_{t+j} \mid w_t)$ is computed via negative sampling as in Equation (2.7).

BiSkip (Luong et al., 2015) uses the same cross-lingual regularization terms as Trans-gram, but only aims to predict monotonically aligned target language words: Each source word at position i in the source sentence $sent^s$ is aligned to the target word at position $i \cdot \frac{|sent^s|}{|sent^t|}$ in the target sentence $sent^t$. In practice, all these bilingual skip-gram models are trained by sampling a pair of aligned sentences from a parallel corpus and minimizing for the source and target language sentence the respective loss terms.

In a similar vein, Pham et al. (2015) propose an extension of paragraph vectors (Le and Mikolov, 2014) to the multilingual setting by forcing aligned sentences of different languages to share the same vector representation.

Other sentence-level approaches   Levy et al. (2017) use another sentence-level bilingual signal: IDs of the aligned sentence pairs in a parallel corpus. Their model provides a strong baseline for cross-lingual word embeddings that is inspired by the Dice Coefficient commonly used for producing word alignments for MT. Observing that sentence IDs are already a powerful bilingual signal, they propose to apply SGNS to the word-sentence ID matrix. They show that this method can be seen as a generalization of the Dice Coefficient.

Rajendran et al. (2016) propose a method that exploits the idea of using pivot languages, also tackled in previous work, e.g., Shezaf and Rappoport (2010). The model requires parallel data between each language and a pivot language and is able to learn a shared embedding space for two languages without any direct alignment signals as the alignment is implicitly learned via their alignment with the pivot language. The model optimizes a correlation term with neural network encoders and decoders that is similar to the objective of the CCA-based approaches (Faruqui and Dyer, 2014, Lu et al., 2015). We discuss the importance of pivoting for learning multilingual word embeddings later in Chapter 8.

6.2   SENTENCE ALIGNMENT WITH COMPARABLE DATA

Similar to approaches based on word-level aligned comparable data, Elliott and Kádár (2017) demonstrate cross-lingual word embeddings from sentences aligned with images. Specifically, they use image captions in different languages (for the same images). The captions are not translations of each other, but obviously very related. Calixto et al. (2017) represent images using features from a pre-trained CNN and model sentences using a GRU. They then use MMHL to assign a higher score to image-description pairs compared to images with a random description. Gella et al. (2017) augment this objective with another MMHL term that also brings the representations of translated descriptions closer together, thus effectively combining learning signals from both visual and textual modality.

CHAPTER 7

Document-Level Alignment Models

If two documents are translations of each other, it is typically possible to align most sentences in these documents with their translations. This means that parallel documents often imply parallel sentences. Comparable document-level alignment, on the other hand, is cheaper to obtain and does not imply sentence-level alignments exist. Existing approaches to inducing cross-lingual word embeddings from such document collections generally use Wikipedia pages, which come aligned by the Wikipedia concept ID tags.

7.1 DOCUMENT ALIGNMENT WITH COMPARABLE DATA

We divide models using document alignment with comparable data into three types, some of which employ similar general ideas to previously discussed word and sentence-level parallel alignment models.

(a) **Approaches based on pseudo-mixed language corpora** automatically construct a pseudo-mixed language corpus containing words from the source and target language by mixing words from document-aligned documents.

(b) **Concept-based methods** leverage information about the distribution of latent topics or concepts in document-aligned data to represent words.

c) **Extensions of sentence-aligned models** extend methods using sentence-aligned parallel data to also work without parallel data.

Pseudo-mixed document-aligned corpora The approach of Vulić and Moens (2016) is similar to the pseudo-mixed language corpora approaches discussed in Chapter 5. In contrast to previous methods, they propose a *Merge and Shuffle* strategy to merge two aligned documents of different languages into a pseudo-mixed language document. This is done by concatenating the documents and then randomly shuffling them by permuting words. The intuition is that as most methods rely on learning word embeddings based on their context, shuffling the documents will lead to robust bilingual contexts for each word. As the shuffling step is completely random, it might lead to sub-optimal configurations.

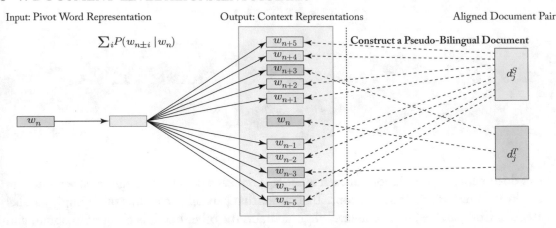

Figure 7.1: The Length-Ratio Shuffle strategy from Vulić and Moens (2016).

For this reason, they propose another strategy for merging the two aligned documents, called *Length-Ratio Shuffle*. It assumes that the structures of the two documents are similar: words are inserted into the pseudo-mixed language document by alternating between the source and the target document relying on the order in which they appear in their monolingual document and based on the monolingual documents' length ratio. The whole process can be seen in Figure 7.1.

Concept-based models   Some methods for learning cross-lingual word embeddings leverage the insight that words in different languages are similar if they are used to talk about or evoke the same multilingual concepts or topics. Vulić and Moens (2013) base their method on the cognitive theory of semantic word responses. Their method centers on the intuition that words in source and target language are similar if they are likely to generate similar words as their top semantic word responses. They utilize a probabilistic multilingual topic model again trained on aligned Wikipedia documents to learn and quantify semantic word responses. The embedding $\mathbf{x}_i^s \in \mathbb{R}^{|V^s|+|V^t|}$ of source word w_i is the following vector:

$$\mathbf{x}_i^s = \left[P(w_1^s|w_i), \dots, P(w_{|V^s|}^s|w_i), P(w_1^t|w_i) \dots, P(w_{|V^t|}^t|w_i) \right], \tag{7.1}$$

where $[\cdot, \cdot]$ represents concatenation and $P(w_j|w_i)$ is the probability of w_j given w_i under the induced bilingual topic model. The sparse representations may be turned into dense vectors by factorizing the constructed word-response matrix.

Søgaard et al. (2015) propose an approach that relies on the structure of Wikipedia itself. Their method is based on the intuition that similar words are used to describe the same concepts across different languages. Instead of representing every Wikipedia concept with the terms that are used to describe it, they use an inverted index and represent a word by the concepts it is used to describe. As a post-processing step, dimensionality reduction on the produced word representations in the word-concept matrix is performed. A very similar model by Vulić et al. (2011) uses a bilingual topic model to perform the dimensionality reduction step and learns a shared cross-lingual topical space.

Extensions of sentence-alignment models   Mogadala and Rettinger (2016) extend the approach of Pham et al. (2015) to also work without parallel data and adjust the regularization term Ω based on the nature of the training corpus. Similar to previous work (Gouws et al., 2015, Hermann and Blunsom, 2013), they use the mean of the word embeddings of a sentence as the sentence representation $\mathbf{y}$ and constrain these to be close together. In addition, they propose to constrain the sentence paragraph vectors $\mathbf{p}^s$ and $\mathbf{p}^t$ of aligned sentences $sent^s$ and $sent^t$ to be close to each other. These vectors are learned via paragraph vectors (Le and Mikolov, 2014) for each sentence and stored in embedding matrices $\mathbf{P}^s$ and $\mathbf{P}^t$. The complete regularizer then uses elastic net regularization to combine both terms:

$$\Omega = \sum_{(sent^s, sent^t) \in C} \alpha ||\mathbf{p}^s - \mathbf{p}^t||^2 + (1 - \alpha)||\mathbf{y}^s - \mathbf{y}^t||^2. \tag{7.2}$$

The monolingual paragraph vector objectives $\mathcal{L}_{\text{SGNS-P}}$ are then optimized jointly with the cross-lingual regularization term:

$$J = \mathcal{L}^s_{\text{SGNS-P}}(\mathbf{P}^s, \mathbf{X}^s) + \mathcal{L}^t_{\text{SGNS-P}}(\mathbf{P}^t, \mathbf{X}^t) + \Omega(\mathbf{P}^s, \mathbf{P}^t, \mathbf{X}^s, \mathbf{X}^t). \tag{7.3}$$

To leverage data that is not sentence-aligned, but where an alignment is still present on the document level, they propose a two-step approach: they use Procrustes Analysis (Schönemann, 1966), a method for statistical shape analysis, to find the most similar document in language t for each document in language s. This is done by first learning monolingual representations of the documents in each language using paragraph vectors on each corpus. Subsequently, Procrustes analysis aims to learn a transformation between the two vector spaces by translating, rotating, and scaling the embeddings in the first space until they most closely align to the document representations in the second space. In the second step, they then simply use the previously described method to learn cross-lingual word representations from the alignment documents, this time treating the entire documents as paragraphs.

CHAPTER 8

From Bilingual to Multilingual Training

So far, we have discussed *bilingual* word embeddings, i.e., cross-lingual word embeddings in a shared space comprising only two languages. However, Levy et al. (2017) and Duong et al. (2017) demonstrate that there are clear benefits to including more languages, moving from bilingual to *multilingual* settings, in which the vocabularies of more than two languages are represented.

The usefulness of multilingual training for NLP is already discussed by, e.g., Naseem et al. (2009) and Snyder and Barzilay (2010). They present a hypothesis that cross-lingual variation in lexical ambiguity is a form of naturally occurring supervision. What one language leaves implicit, another defines explicitly, and alignment with multiple other languages can help resolve different ambiguities (Faruqui and Dyer, 2014). Using multiple languages improves the quality of this implicit supervision, which in turn leads to better word embedding estimates (Mrkšić et al., 2017). Note that even when learning one-to-one mappings of vocabularies, the differences in the distribution over senses over the vocabularies of multiple languages may act as an efficient regularizer. This is also the motivation behind multi-source cross-lingual transfer, for example McDonald et al. (2011).

In most previous work on learning bilingual word embeddings, English is typically the target language. This of course introduces a bias, and is the reason that cross-lingual word embeddings are best when the source language is typologically similar to English. In other words, learning cross-lingual word embeddings for English-Nahuatl may—all things being equal—be harder than learning cross-lingual word embeddings for Quechua–Nahuatl, because Quechua and Nahuatl are typologically more similar than with English. Now in practice, all things are not equal, and we may not have a lot of supervision for learning a mapping between Quechua and Nahuatl word embeddings, for example. Question is, however, if we can get the best of both worlds by learning multi-lingual word embeddings for English, Nahuatl, *and* Quechua?

In this chapter, we briefly present a few multilingual word embedding models, again following the typology of models established in Table 3.1.

8.1 MULTILINGUAL WORD EMBEDDINGS FROM WORD-LEVEL INFORMATION

Mapping-based approaches   We begin with probably the simplest possible approach to learning multilingual word embeddings: namely, mapping several source languages into the same space, e.g., an English word embedding space. Mapping L different monolingual spaces into a single multilingual shared space is achieved by: (1) selecting one space as the *pivot space*, and then (2) mapping the remaining $L - 1$ spaces into the same pivot space. This approach, illustrated by Figure 8.1, requires L monolingual spaces and $L - 1$ seed translation dictionaries to achieve the mapping.

Labeling the pivot language as l^p, we can formulate the induction of a multilingual word embedding space as follows:

$$\mathcal{L}^1 + \mathcal{L}^2 + \ldots + \mathcal{L}^{L-1} + \mathcal{L}^p + \Omega^{l^1 \to l^p} + \Omega^{l^2 \to l^p} + \ldots + \Omega^{l^{L-1} \to l^p}. \tag{8.1}$$

This means that through *pivoting* one is able to induce a shared bilingual space for a language pair without having any directly usable bilingual resources for the pair. Exactly this multilingual mapping procedure (based on minimizing Ω_{MSE}) has been constructed by Smith et al. (2017): 89 other languages are mapped into the pivot English space. Seed translation pairs are obtained through Google Translate API by translating the 5,000 most frequent words in each language to English. Whether this approach scales to language pairs for which supervision is rare, is unclear; see Chapter 9. Smith et al. (2017) use original fastText vectors available in 90 languages (Bojanowski et al., 2017)[1] and effectively construct a multilingual word embedding space spanning 90 languages (i.e., 4005 language pairs using 89 seed translation dictionaries) in their software and experiments.[2] The distances in all monolingual spaces remain preserved by constraining the transformation to be orthogonal.

Along the same line, Ammar et al. (2016b) introduce a multilingual extension of the CCA-based mapping approach. They perform a multilingual extension of bilingual CCA projection for L languages using the English embedding space as the pivot for multiple *English*-to-foreign-language bilingual CCA projections with the remaining $L - 1$ languages.

As demonstrated by Smith et al. (2017), the multilingual space now enables reasoning for language pairs not represented in the seed lexicon data. They verify this hypothesis by examining the bilingual lexicon induction task for all $\binom{L}{2}$ language pairs, e.g., BLI Precision-at-one ($P@1$) scores[3] or Spanish–Catalan without any seed Spanish–Catalan lexicon are 0.82, while the average $P@1$ score for Spanish–English and Catalan–English bilingual spaces is 0.70. Other

---

[1]The latest release of fastText vectors contains vectors for 204 languages. The vectors are available here: https://github.com/facebookresearch/fastText.

[2]https://github.com/Babylonpartners/fastText_multilingual

[3] $P@1$ is a standard evaluation measure for bilingual lexicon induction that refers to the proportion of source test words for which the best translation is ranked as the most similar word in the target language.

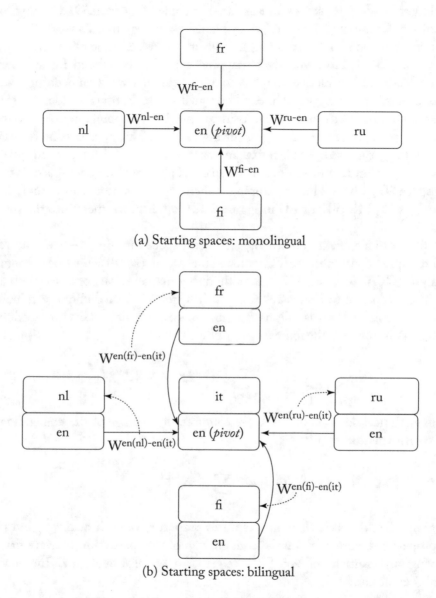

Figure 8.1: Learning shared multilingual word embedding spaces via linear mapping. (a) Starting from monolingual spaces in L languages, one linearly maps $L - 1$ into one chosen pivot monolingual space (typically English); and (b) starting from bilingual spaces sharing a language (typically English), one learns mappings from all other English subspaces into one chosen pivot English subspace and then applies the mapping to all other subspaces.

striking findings include $P@1$ scores for Russian–Ukrainian (0.84 vs. 0.59), Czech–Slovak (0.82 vs. 0.59), Serbian–Croatian (0.78 vs. 0.56), or Danish–Norwegian (0.73 vs. 0.67).

A similar approach to constructing a multilingual word embedding space is discussed by Duong et al. (2017). However, their mapping approach is tailored for another scenario frequently encountered in practice: one has to align bilingual word embedding spaces where English is one of the two languages in each bilingual space. In other words, our starting embedding spaces are now not monolingual as in the previous mapping approach, but bilingual. The overview of the approach is also given in Figure 8.1b. This approach first selects a pivot bilingual space (e.g., this is th English–Italian space in Figure 8.1b), and then learns a linear mapping/transformation from the English subspace of all other bilingual spaces into the pivot English subspace. The learned linear mapping is then applied to other subspaces (i.e., "foreign" subspaces such as FI, FR, NL, or RU in Figure 8.1b) to transform them into the shared multilingual space.

Projecting into a specific (often English) vector space introduces a bias, and researchers have therefore explored alternatives. Kementchedjhieva et al. (2018) show that Generalized Procrustes Analysis (GPA) (Gower, 1975), a method that maps two vector spaces into a third, latent space ($\mathbf{X}^l$), is superior to Procrustes Analysis (PA) for bilingual dictionary induction. GPA is a natural extension of PA that aligns k vector spaces at a time. Given embedding spaces $\mathbf{X}^1, \ldots, \mathbf{X}^k$, GPA minimizes the following objective:

$$\arg \min_{\{\mathbf{W}^{1 \to l}, \ldots, \mathbf{W}^{k \to l}\}} \sum_{i<j}^{k} \left\| \mathbf{W}^{i \to l} \mathbf{X}^i - \mathbf{W}_j^{j \to l} \mathbf{X}^j \right\|^2. \tag{8.2}$$

For an analytical solution to GPA, we compute the average of the embedding matrices $\mathbf{X}^{1 \ldots k}$ after transformation by $\mathbf{W}^{1 \ldots k \to l}$:

$$G = k^{-1} \sum_{i=1}^{k} \mathbf{X}^i \mathbf{W}^{i \to l}, \tag{8.3}$$

thus, obtaining a latent space, G, which captures properties of each of $\mathbf{X}^{1 \ldots k}$, and potentially additional properties emerging from the combination of the spaces. On the very first iteration, prior to having any estimates of $\mathbf{W}^{1 \ldots k \to l}$, we set $G = \mathbf{X}^i$ for a random i. The new values of $\mathbf{W}^{1 \ldots k \to l}$ are then obtained as:

$$\begin{aligned} G^\top \mathbf{X}^i &= U \Sigma V^\top \\ \mathbf{W}^{i \to l} &= V U^\top \text{ for } i \text{ in } 1 \ldots k. \end{aligned} \tag{8.4}$$

Since G is dependent on $\mathbf{W}^{1 \ldots k \to l}$ (see Equation (8.3)), the solution of GPA cannot be obtained in a single step (as is the case with PA), but rather requires that we loop over subsequent updates of G (Equation (8.3)) and $\mathbf{W}^{1 \ldots k \to l}$ (Equation (8.4)) for a fixed number of steps or until satisfactory convergence.

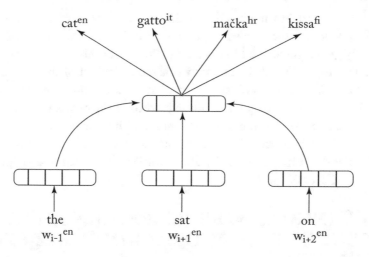

Figure 8.2: Illustration of the joint multilingual model of Duong et al. (2017) based on the modified CBOW objective; instead of predicting only the English word given the English context, the model also tries to predict its translations in all the remaining languages (i.e., in languages for which translations exist in any of the input bilingual lexicons).

Doval et al. (2018) present a very similar technique, but aligning aligned word pairs to their average only after an initial alignment has been computed. It is an open question whether this approach is equivalent, superior, or inferior to the approach in Kementchedjhieva et al. (2018).

○ **Open Problem**   What is the best way of aligning word vector spaces into a latent, common space that spans multiple (typologically diverse) languages?

Pseudo-mixed and joint approaches   Joint multilingual models rely on exactly the same input data (i.e., monolingual data plus multiple bilingual dictionaries) and the core idea is again to exploit multilingual word contexts. An extension of the *joint* modeling paradigm to multilingual settings, illustrated in Figure 8.2, is discussed by Duong et al. 2017. The core model is an extension of their bilingual model (Duong et al., 2016) based on the CBOW-style objective: in the multilingual scenario with L languages, for each language l^i the training procedure consists of predicting the center word in language l^i given the monolingual context in l^i plus predicting all translations of the center word in all other languages, subject to their presence in the input bilingual dictionaries. Note that effectively this MultiCBOW model may be seen as a combination of multiple monolingual and cross-lingual CBOW-style sub-objectives as follows:

$$J = \mathcal{L}^1_{\text{CBOW}} + \mathcal{L}^2_{\text{CBOW}} + \cdots + \mathcal{L}^L_{\text{CBOW}} + \mathcal{L}^{1\rightarrow2}_{\text{CBOW}} + \mathcal{L}^{2\rightarrow1}_{\text{CBOW}} + \cdots \mathcal{L}^{(L-1)\rightarrow L}_{\text{CBOW}} + \mathcal{L}^{L\rightarrow(L-1)}_{\text{CBOW}}, \quad (8.5)$$

where the cross-lingual part of the objective again serves as the cross-lingual regularizer Ω. By replacing the CBOW-style objective with the SGNS objective, the model described by Equation (8.5) effectively gets transformed to the straightforward multilingual extension of the bilingual BiSkip model (Luong et al., 2015). Exactly this model, called MultiSkip, is described in the work of Ammar et al. 2016b. Instead of summing contexts around the center word as in CBOW, the model now tries to predict surrounding context words of the center word in its own language, plus its translations and all surrounding context words of its translations in all other languages. Translations are again obtained from input dictionaries or extracted from word alignments as in the original BiSkip and MultiSkip models. The pivot language idea is also applicable with the MultiSkip and MultiCBOW models.

8.2   MULTILINGUAL WORD EMBEDDINGS FROM SENTENCE-LEVEL AND DOCUMENT-LEVEL INFORMATION

Extending bilingual word embedding models which learn on the basis of aligned sentences and documents closely follows the principles already established for word-level models in Chapter 8.1. For instance, the multilingual extension of the Trans-gram model from Coulmance et al. (2015) may be seen as MultiSkip without word alignment information (see again Table 6.1). In other words, instead of predicting only words in the neighborhood of the word aligned to the center word, TransGram predicts all words in the sentences aligned to the sentence which contains the current center word (i.e., the model assumes uniform word alignment). This idea is illustrated by Figure 8.3. English is again used as the pivot language to reduce bilingual data requirements.

The same idea of pivoting, that is, learning multiple bilingual spaces linked through the shared pivot English space is directly applicable to other prominent bilingual word embedding models (Chandar et al., 2014, Gouws et al., 2015, Hermann and Blunsom, 2014, Soyer et al., 2015, Zou et al., 2013).

The document-level model of Vulić et al. (2016) may be extended to the multilingual setting using the same idea as in previously discussed word-level pseudo-multilingual approaches. Søgaard et al. (2015) and Levy et al. (2017) exploit the structure of a multi-comparable Wikipedia dataset and a multi-parallel Bible dataset respectively to directly build sparse cross-lingual representations using the same set of shared indices (i.e., the former uses the indices of aligned Wikipedia articles while the latter relies on the indices of aligned sentences in the multi-parallel corpus). Dense word embeddings are then obtained by factorizing the multilingual word-concept matrix containing all words from all vocabularies.

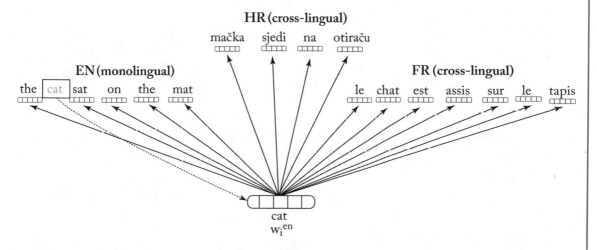

Figure 8.3: A multilingual extension of the sentence-level TransGram model of Coulmance et al. (2015). Since the model bypasses the word alignment step in its SGNS-style objective, for each center word (e.g., the EN word *cat* in this example) the model predicts *all* words in each sentence (from all other languages) which is aligned to the current sentence (e.g., the EN sentence *the cat sat on the mat*).

CHAPTER 9

Unsupervised Learning of Cross-Lingual Word Embeddings

In the context of mapping-based approaches, there has been a lot of work showing much less supervision is needed to learn reliable projections than what was previously assumed. Vulić and Moens (2016) were first to show this, and Artetxe et al. (2017), Smith et al. (2017), and Søgaard et al. (2018) explored using even weaker supervision signals, including, numerals and words that are identical across languages. Several authors have recently proposed entirely *unsupervised* approaches to learning cross-lingual word embeddings by projecting word vector spaces onto each other, based, for example, on Generative Adversarial Networks (GANs) (Goodfellow et al., 2014) or iterative closest point (ICP) algorithms (Hoshen and Wolf, 2018), both of which were originally developed to solve problems in computer vision. We present the core idea behind these approaches below, but briefly put, these algorithms learn a linear transformation to minimize the divergence between a target distribution (say, Icelandic embeddings) and a source distribution (English embeddings projected into the Icelandic space). We also briefly discuss their limitations and some alternative techniques.

Most approaches to unsupervised learning of cross-lingual word embeddings are, however, *two-step approaches*, and GANs or ICP, for example, are what is used in the first step. In this step, what is typically produced is a seed dictionary. In the second step, this seed dictionary is used to supervise a standard mapping algorithm; such as Procrustes Analysis (Schönemann, 1966) or any of the alternatives listed in Chapter 5. In between the two steps, there is an important heuristic; namely, how word pairs are extracted to build the seed dictionary. We discuss the seed dictionary induction strategies in Section 9.1 and, briefly, the second refinement step and the associated heuristics in Section 9.2. Note we also used this three-way terminology to discuss supervised approaches based on word alignments in Chapter 5, but as we said then, refinement and heuristics are particularly important for unsupervised methods.

Recent results with unsupervised methods have been very promising, in a few cases superseding the performance of supervised methods (Artetxe et al., 2018b, Conneau et al., 2018). Yet, it remains an open question whether the initial, positive results extrapolate to real-world scenarios of learning cross-lingual word embeddings for low-resource language pairs. Søgaard et al. (2018), for example, presented results suggesting that some unsupervised learning algorithms are challenged by language pairs exhibiting very different morpho-syntactic properties, as well as when the monolingual corpora are very different. We survey these results in Section 9.3, as well as those in Artetxe et al. (2018b), Hartmann et al. (2018), and Nakashole and Flauger (2018). It is important to note, however, that this chapter comes with the important disclaimer that unsupervised learning of cross-lingual word embeddings is a crowded area these days, with new algorithms being presented every month. Our overview is therefore necessarily incomplete at the time you read this book; and moreover, many of the algorithms we cover have not yet stood the test of time and their limitations are only partially understood.

9.1   SEED DICTIONARY INDUCTION

The most interesting step in unsupervised learning of cross-lingual word embeddings is arguably the seed dictionary induction step. For many, the observation that unsupervised learning of cross-lingual word embeddings is possible, at least under some circumstances, is counter-intuitive, and it is this first step that, to some, seems almost magical. It does not follow, of course, that this is also the step that does most of the work. The first time a child flies on an airplane, take-off is what seems magical, albeit only a small fraction of the journey. In experiments run by the authors of this book, we have often observed that refinement and heuristics have turned seemingly very poor seed dictionaries into very useful cross-lingual word embeddings, pushing precision scores from close to 0 to higher than 0.5.

GENERATIVE ADVERSARIAL NETWORKS

The seminal paper using GANs for seed dictionary induction is Barone (2016), but Zhang et al. (2017a) and Conneau et al. (2018) quickly followed. Both Barone (2016) and Conneau et al. (2018) use a vanilla GAN with a linear generator to learn alignments between embedding spaces. In a two-player game, a discriminator D aims to tell the two embedding spaces apart, while a generator G aims to fool the discriminator by mapping the source language space onto the target language space. The generator G is therefore trained to fool the discriminator D. This is done by letting the generator peak at the losses the discriminator suffers. The generator can be any differentiable function, but in our context, it will be a linear transformation $\mathbf{W}^{s \to t}$. Let our source language s be French, and our target language t be English. $\mathbf{x}^s \in \mathbf{X}^s$ is a French word vector, and $\mathbf{x}^t \in \mathbf{X}^t$ a English word vector. The goal of the generator is to choose $\mathbf{W}^{s \to t}$ such that its output $\mathbf{W}^{s \to t}\mathbf{X}^s$ has a distribution close to $\mathbf{X}^t$. The generator presents the discriminator with $\mathbf{W}^{s \to t}(\mathbf{e})$. The discriminator is a map $D_w : \mathcal{X} \to \{0, 1\}$; in the experiments of Conneau et al. (2018), a multi-layered perceptron. The job of the discriminator is to discriminate between vectors $\mathbf{X}^t$ and $\mathbf{W}^{s \to t}\mathbf{X}^s$. Since for any vector $\mathbf{x}$, we know whether $\mathbf{x} \in \mathbf{X}^s$ or $\mathbf{x} \in \mathbf{X}^t$, we can compute the loss of the discriminator on a batch of N samples from $\mathbf{X}^s$ and N samples from $\mathbf{X}^t$ and update it accordingly:

$$w \rightarrow w + \alpha \sum_{i=1}^{N} \nabla \left[\log D_w \left(\mathbf{X}_i^t \right) + \log \left(1 - D_w \left(\mathbf{W}^{s \rightarrow t} \left(\mathbf{X}_i^s \right) \right) \right) \right].$$

The loss of the generator will be derived from the loss of the discriminator, since the job of the generator is to fool the discriminator, and the loss of the generator is therefore the inverse of the loss of the discriminator.

The parameters of the GAN are $(\mathbf{W}^{s \rightarrow t}, w)$. They are obtained by solving the following min-max problem:

$$\min_{\mathbf{W}^{s \rightarrow t}} \max_{w} \mathrm{E} \left[\log \left(D_w \left(\mathbf{X}^t \right) \right) + \log \left(1 - D_w \left(g_{\mathbf{W}}^{s \rightarrow t} \left(\mathbf{X}^s \right) \right) \right) \right], \tag{9.1}$$

which reduces to

$$\min_{\Omega} JS \left(P_{\mathbf{X}^r} \mid P_{\mathbf{W}^{s \rightarrow t}} \right). \tag{9.2}$$

If a generator wins the game against an ideal discriminator on a very large number of samples, then $\mathbf{X}^t$ and $\mathbf{W}^{s \rightarrow t} \mathbf{X}^s$ can be shown to be close in Jensen–Shannon divergence (Goodfellow et al., 2014) and, thus, the model has learned the true distribution. This result, referring to the distributions of the data, p_{data}, and the distribution, p_g, G is sampling from, is from Goodfellow et al. (2014).

Lemma 9.1 *If G and D have enough capacity, and at each step of training, the discriminator is allowed to reach its optimum given G, and p_g is updated so as to improve the criterion*

$$E_{\mathbf{x} \sim p_{data}} \left[\log D_G^* (\mathbf{x}) \right] + E_{\mathbf{x} \sim p_g} \left[\log \left(1 - D_G^* (\mathbf{x}) \right) \right]$$

then p_g converges to p_{data}.

This result relies on a number of assumptions that do not hold in practice, of course. Our generator, which learns a linear transform Ω, has very limited capacity, for example, and we are updating Ω rather than p_g. In practice, therefore, during training, we alternate between k steps of optimizing the discriminator and one step of optimizing the generator. While sometimes this is sufficient in practice, the limitations of vanilla GANs in our context remains an open question.

Instability   While Conneau et al. (2018) and related systems have achieved impressive results at times, they are also highly unstable, e.g., with different initializations leading to precision scores that vary between 0% and 45% for English–Greek (Søgaard et al., 2018). See Artetxe et al. (2018b) for more experiments. This is a general problem when training GANs. Nagarajan and Kolter (2017) show, however, that GANs with linear discriminators are locally stable. Heusel et al. (2017) show that GANs trained with a two-time scale update rule are also locally stable. Other work has replaced the Jensen-Shannon objective of GANs with other objectives that prove more stable, including Wasserstein distance (Arjovsky et al., 2017) and a Fisher integral probability metric (Mroueh and Sercu, 2017). Wasserstein GANs were used for learning cross-lingual word embeddings in Zhang et al. (2017a), but so far, no one has to the best of our knowledge presented a systematic comparison of the instability of these two seed dictionary induction algorithms. We briefly discuss Wasserstein GANs and related algorithms below.

ITERATIVE CLOSEST POINT

Unsupervised learning of cross-lingual word embeddings through mapping is a point set registration problem (Gold et al., 1998). In the point set registration literature, ICP is very often used as a baseline approach to aligning point sets. Just like GANs, ICP is very sensitive to initialization, and it is interesting that a lot of applications of point set registration rely on initialization strategies using a few gold standard alignments or manual evaluation of random restarts, e.g., Darkner et al. (2006). This blurs the distinction between unsupervised and supervised approaches to point set registration—or learning cross-lingual word embeddings. Unsupervised initialization strategies have also been proposed in the computer vision literature, e.g., Haddad et al. (2016).

Iterative closest point (ICP) optimization (Besl and McKay, 1992) explicitly minimizes the ℓ_2 distance (mean squared error) between nearest neighbor pairs. The ICT optimization algorithm works by assigning each transformed vector to its nearest neighbor and then computing the new relative transformation that minimizes the cost function with respect to this assignment. ICP can be shown to converge to local optima (Besl and McKay, 1992), in polynomial time (Ezra et al., 2006). ICP easily gets trapped in local optima, however, and exact algorithms only exist for two- and three-dimensional point set registration, and those algorithms are slow (Yang et al., 2016). Generally, it holds that the optimal solution to the minmax problem in Equation (9.1) is also optimal for ICP. To see this note that a GAN minimizes the Jensen–Shannon divergence between $\mathbf{X}^t$ and $\mathbf{W}^{s \to t}\mathbf{X}^s$ (Goodfellow et al., 2014). The optimal solution to this is $\mathbf{X}^t = \mathbf{W}^{s \to t}\mathbf{X}^s$. As sample size goes to infinite, this means the $\mathcal{L}_2$ loss in ICP goes to 0. In other words, ICP loss is minimal if an optimal solution to the GAN problem is found. ICP was independently proposed for unsupervised learning of cross-lingual word embeddings in Hoshen and Wolf (2018). Interestingly, they report their method only works using PCA for dimensionality reduction; see Section 10.2.

OTHER SEED DICTIONARY INDUCTION TECHNIQUES

While vanilla GANs and ICP serve as good reference points for an overview of recent work on seed dictionary induction, several papers have introduced alternatives over the last two years. Here, we briefly summarize the Wasserstein GAN lineage of such alternatives, as well as work on more explicitly applying graph matching algorithms.

Wasserstein GAN   Zhang et al. (2017a) use a Wasserstein GAN (Arjovsky et al., 2017) instead of a vanilla GAN. Minimizing the GAN objective function with an optimal discriminator is equivalent to minimizing the JS-divergence between $\mathbf{X}^s$ and $\mathbf{X}^t$, and when $\mathbf{X}^s = \mathbf{X}^t$, divergence is 0. However, as the divergence increases, gradients eventually diminish, and the generator learns nothing from the gradient descent. This is commonly referred to as *mode collapse*, and one motivation behind the Wasserstein GAN objective, which has a smoother gradient everywhere, is to reduce the instability caused by mode collapses. The Wasserstein distance is the minimum cost of transporting mass in converting the data distribution $\mathbf{X}^s$ to the data distribution $\mathbf{X}^t$. This leads to almost linear gradients, in sharp contrast with vanilla GANs. Another motivation for using Wasserstein GANs is also to avoid hubs (Dinu et al., 2015, Radovanović et al., 2010) in the cross-lingual word embedding space. In the MUSE system presented by Conneau et al. (2018), they use heuristics (so-called *cross-domain local similarity scaling*) to prevent hubs instead. We discuss this system and the heuristics used in it in Section 9.2.

From WGANs to CT-GANs   Several extensions of Wasserstein GANs now exist: WGANs with gradient penalty (Gulrajani et al., 2017), for example, introduce a form of gradient regularization, motivated by the observation that WGAN training requires heuristic gradient clipping with undesirable behaviors: specifically, in WGANs with gradient penalty, the norm of the discriminator gradients is regularized to be at most 1 everywhere, which stabilizes training. CT-GANs (Wei et al., 2018) were subsequently proposed as an improvement over WGANs with gradient penalty. Instead of relying on gradient clipping or gradient regularization, CT-GANs rely on implicit data augmentation. In particular, they perturb each real data point twice and use a Lipschitz constant to bound the difference between the discriminator's responses to the perturbed data points. Both approaches to training can be seen as regularizing the induction of Wasserstein GANs. Unnormalized Wasserstein distance with entropic regularization (known as Sinkhorn distance) was used for unsupervised learning of cross-lingual word embeddings in Xu et al. (2018).

Graph matching   Aligning two sets of monolingual word embeddings can also be seen as a graph matching problem (von der Malsburg, 1988). The exact graph matching problem can be formulated as follows: given two graphs $G_i = (V_i, E_i)$ and $G_j = (V_j, E_j)$, with $|V_i| = |V_j|$, the problem is to find a one-to-one mapping $f : V_j \rightarrow V_i$ such that $(u, v) \in E_j$ if and only if $(f(u), f(v)) \in E_i$. When such a mapping f exists, this is called an isomorphism, and G_j is said to be isomorphic to G_i. This problem is NP-complete. The same holds for the problem of computing graph edit distance, by the way.

The Gold–Rangarajan relaxation is a convex relaxation of the graph matching problem and can be solved using the Frank–Wolfe algorithm. Once the minimal optimizer is computed, an initial transformation is obtained using singular-value decomposition. The Gold–Rangarajan relaxation can thus, be used for learning of seed dictionaries (Grave et al., 2018). It remains an open question how this strategy fairs on challenging language pairs. Note that other work using graph matching algorithms sometimes have relied on *hand-coded* graphs, i.e., multilingual knowledge bases, whether they have used supervision or not (Wang et al., 2018).

○ **Open Problem**   Is the approach in Grave et al. (2018) robust across language pairs?

9.2   REFINEMENT AND HEURISTICS

As mentioned, most approaches to unsupervised learning of cross-lingual word embeddings are two-step approaches that first induce a seed dictionary and then use a supervised learning algorithm to learn the final embeddings. The second step is sometimes referred to as *refinement*. One notable exception is Barone (2016), a seminal paper on unsupervised learning of cross-lingual word embeddings and one of the only not to include a refinement step.

For refinement, we can use any of the above supervised methods that rely on word alignments. In practice, many researchers have used Procrustes Analysis (see Chapter 5). One reason is the influence of the MUSE system (Conneau et al., 2018). Because of its influence, we briefly describe this approach first, including heuristics used in this system. We then go on to describe alternatives to Procrustes Analysis that are used in the unsupervised literature, but not covered in Chapter 5: maximum mean discrepancy (MMD) and the Sinkhorn algorithm. Finally, we discuss a few other heuristics employed in the literature, including stochastic dictionary induction (Artetxe et al., 2018b).

MUSE   MUSE is the system introduced in Conneau et al. (2018). It trains a vanilla GAN to learn a linear transformation of the target language word embeddings into the source language space and extract a seed dictionary using various heuristics. It uses this dictionary to learn a mapping using Procrustes analysis (see Chapter 5). MUSE thus, consists of the following steps.

(1) *Monolingual word embeddings:* an off-the-shelf word embedding algorithm (Bojanowski et al., 2017) is used to learn source and target language spaces $\mathbf{X}^s$ and $\mathbf{X}^t$.

(2) *Adversarial mapping:* a translation matrix Ω is learned between the spaces $\mathbf{X}^s$ and $\mathbf{X}^t$. A discriminator is trained to discriminate samples from the translated source space $\mathbf{W}^{s \to t} \mathbf{X}^s$ from the target space $\mathbf{X}^t$, while $\mathbf{W}^{s \to t}$ is trained to prevent this. This, again, is motivated by the assumption that source and target language word embeddings are approximately isomorphic.

(3) *Refinement (Procrustes analysis):* Ω is used to build a small bilingual dictionary of frequent words, which is pruned such that only bidirectional translations are kept (Vulić et al., 2015). A new translation matrix Ω that translates between the spaces $\mathbf{X}^s$ and $\mathbf{X}^t$ of these frequent word pairs is then induced by solving the Orthogonal Procrustes problem:

$$\Omega^* = \operatorname{argmin}_{\mathbf{W}}^{s \to t} \left\| \mathbf{W}^{s \to t} \mathbf{X}^s - \mathbf{X}^t \right\|_{\text{Frob}} = U V^\top$$
$$\text{s.t. } U \Sigma V^\top = \text{SVD}\left(\mathbf{X}^t \left(\mathbf{X}^s \right)^\top \right). \tag{9.3}$$

This step can be used iteratively by using the new matrix Ω to create new seed translation pairs. It requires frequent words to serve as reliable anchors for learning a translation matrix. In the experiments in Conneau et al. (2018), the iterative Procrustes refinement improves performance across the board.

(4) *Cross-domain similarity local scaling* (CSLS) is used to expand high-density areas and condense low-density ones, for more accurate nearest neighbor calculation, and CSLS thereby reduces the hubness problem in high-dimensional spaces, mentioned above. CSLS, also discussed in Chapter 5, is computed as follows:

$$\text{CSLS}\left(\mathbf{W}\mathbf{x}^s, \mathbf{x}^t\right) = 2\cos\left(\mathbf{W}\mathbf{x}^s, \mathbf{x}^t\right) - r^t\left(\mathbf{W}\mathbf{x}^s\right) - r^s\left(\mathbf{x}^t\right), \qquad (9.4)$$

where r^t is the mean similarity of a target word to its neighborhood, defined as $r^t\left(\mathbf{W}\mathbf{x}_s\right) = \frac{1}{K}\sum_{\mathbf{x}_t \in \mathcal{N}^t(\mathbf{W}\mathbf{x}^s)} \cos(\mathbf{W}\mathbf{x}^s, \mathbf{x}^t)$ where $\mathcal{N}^t\left(\mathbf{W}\mathbf{x}^s\right)$ is the neighborhood of the projected source word.

MMD   Yang et al. (2018) use the kernel trick to explicitly minimize the maximum mean discrepancy (MMD). In order to estimate the maximum discrepancy between the vector spaces through sampling, they project both into low-dimensional space. They use the initialization strategy in Artetxe et al. (2018a). Note MMD was previously introduced for other tasks, including domain adaptation (Yoshikawa et al., 2015) and semi-supervised machine translation (Hamilton, 2018).

Stochastic dictionary induction and other heuristics   Artetxe et al. (2018b) introduce a very simple heuristic that seems to be why they achieve relatively robust performance. They call the heuristic *stochastic dictionary induction*, and it works as follows: the seed dictionary after the unsupervised learning step is extracted from a similarity matrix. Artetxe et al. (2018b) randomly delete elements of this matrix with probability $1 - p$. This is also done in between subsequent iterations of Procrustes Analysis. The smaller the value of p is, the more the induced dictionary will vary. The motivation behind this variance is to escape local optima. Artetxe et al. (2018b) therefore increase p over the course of these iterations, akin to simulated annealing, starting with $p = 0.1$ and doubling this value every time the loss has not gone down for a while. Hoshen and Wolf (2018) preprocess their data using principled component analysis before they apply ICP; this form of compression can lead to speed-ups and more robust performance, but at least one of the authors of this book has observed degradation in performance in combination with other seed induction algorithms (GANs). Hoshen and Wolf (2018) also use random restarts and an unsupervised model selection criterion—in a way similar to the stopping criterion in MUSE—as a heuristic. Finally, Xu et al. (2018) provide projections in both direction and add a back-translation loss to their objective.

○ **Open Problem**   How do other seed dictionary induction algorithms perform in the context of stochastic dictionary induction (Artetxe et al., 2018b)?

9.3   LIMITATIONS OF UNSUPERVISED APPROACHES

Several authors have already discussed some apparent limitations of the above unsupervised approaches.

Søgaard et al. (2018) identify three limitations of the MUSE system: (a) MUSE does not reliably induce good alignments for all pairs of languages, e.g., when one language is morphologically rich and dependency-marking; (b) MUSE does not reliably align embeddings induced from different domains; and (c) MUSE does not reliably align embeddings induced using different algorithms. MUSE, for example, near-perfectly aligns English-Spanish embeddings induced using FastText on sizeable Wikipedia dumps, but fails to align such embeddings for English and Estonian. MUSE also fails to align embeddings learned from English medical corpora with Spanish Wikipedia embeddings; or embeddings learned using different word embedding algorithms. Søgaard et al. (2018) note that for the challenging language pairs, MUSE, whose discriminator parameters are randomly initialized, sometimes learns reasonable embeddings, but only in rare cases.

Artetxe et al. (2018b) quantify this instability and show that for Italian, for example, they induce good alignments in 2/10 cases; for Turkish, it is 5/10 cases. Artetxe et al. (2018b) also present an alternative method that seems more robust.

In some of the cases discussed in Søgaard et al. (2018) and Artetxe et al. (2018b), GANs fail because of mode collapse (Goodfellow et al., 2014), but in other cases, they may fail because there is no linear mapping (Nakashole and Flauger, 2018). Hartmann et al. (2018) identify a pathological class of alignment problems where GANs fail miserably, although it is clear that a near-perfect linear alignment exists. In particular, Hartmann et al. (2018) found that GANs can reliably align embeddings that are learned on two different samples of the English Wikipedia, but only if these embeddings are learned using the same word embedding algorithm. For every attempt to align embeddings learned using different embedding algorithms (even if trained on the same Wikipedia sample), unsupervised alignment using a GAN fails. This is interesting, as perfect alignment results using (supervised) Procrustes Analysis shows that a linear mapping between these embeddings exists. The authors hypothesize that inductive biases of the different word embedding algorithms lead to non-convex loss surfaces, but leave it as an open problem to establish this claim or get a deeper understanding of the problem. Note that Søgaard et al. (2018) had already shown that two embeddings in different languages *and* induced with different algorithms were hard to align.

○ **Open Problem**   Why do vanilla GANs fail on the examples in Hartmann et al. (2018)?

CHAPTER 10

Applications and Evaluation

Given the wide array of cross-lingual models and their potential applications, there is an equally wide array of possible evaluation settings. In the following, we discuss the most common intrinsic and extrinsic evaluation tasks that have been used to test cross-lingual word embeddings and outline associated challenges.

10.1 INTRINSIC EVALUATION

The first two widely used tasks are *intrinsic* evaluation tasks: they evaluate cross-lingual word embeddings in a controlled *in vitro* setting that is geared toward revealing certain characteristics of the representations. The major downside with these tasks is that good performance on them does not generalize necessarily to good performance on downstream tasks (Schnabel et al., 2015, Tsvetkov et al., 2016).

Word similarity This task evaluates how well the notion of word similarity according to humans is emulated in the vector space. Multi-lingual word similarity datasets are multilingual extensions of datasets that have been used for evaluating English word representations. Many of these originate from psychology research and consist of word pairs—ranging from synonyms (e.g., car–automobile) to unrelated terms (e.g., noon–string)—that have been annotated with a relatedness score by human subjects. The most commonly used ones of these human judgement datasets are: (a) the RG dataset (Rubenstein and Goodenough, 1965); (b) the MC dataset (Miller and Charles, 1991); (c) the WordSim-353 dataset (Finkelstein et al., 2002), a superset of MC; and (d) the SimLex-999 dataset (Hill et al., 2015). Extending them to the multilingual setting then mainly involves translating the word pairs into different languages: WordSim-353 has been translated to Spanish, Romanian, and Arabic (Hassan and Mihalcea, 2009) and to German, Italian, and Russian (Leviant and Reichart, 2015); RG was translated to German (Gurevych, 2005), French, (Joubarne and Inkpen, 2011), Spanish and Farsi (Camacho-Collados et al., 2015); and SimLex-999 was translated to German, Italian and Russian (Leviant and Reichart, 2015) and to Hebrew and Croatian (Mrkšić et al., 2017). Other prominent datasets for word embedding evaluation such as MEN (Bruni et al., 2014), RareWords (Luong et al., 2013), and SimVerb-3500 (Gerz et al., 2016) have only been used in monolingual contexts.

The SemEval 2017 task on cross-lingual and multilingual word similarity (Camacho-Collados et al., 2017) has introduced cross-lingual word similarity datasets between five languages: English, German, Italian, Spanish, and Farsi, yielding 10 new datasets in total. Each cross-lingual dataset is of reasonable size, containing between 888 and 978 word pairs.

Cross-lingual word similarity datasets are affected by the same problems as their monolingual variants (Faruqui et al., 2016), as shown in Bakarov et al. (2018): the annotated notion of word similarity is subjective and is often confused with relatedness; the datasets evaluate semantic rather than task-specific similarity, which is arguably more useful; they do not have standardized splits; they correlate only weakly with performance on downstream tasks; past models do not use statistical significance; and they do not account for polysemy, which is even more important in the cross-lingual setting.

multiQVEC+   multiQVEC+ is a multilingual extension of QVEC (Tsvetkov et al., 2015), a method that seeks to quantify the linguistic content of word embeddings by maximizing the correlation with a manually-annotated linguistic resource. A semantic linguistic matrix is first constructed from a semantic database. The word embedding matrix is then aligned with the linguistic matrix and the correlation is measured using cumulative dimension-wise correlation. Ammar et al. (2016b) propose QVEC+, which computes correlation using CCA and extend QVEC to the multilingual setting (multiQVEC) by using supersense tag annotations in multiple languages to construct the linguistic matrix. While QVEC has been shown to correlate well with certain semantic downstream tasks, as an intrinsic evaluation task it can only approximately capture the performance as it relates to downstream tasks.

10.2 EXTRINSIC EVALUATION THROUGH CROSS-LINGUAL TRANSFER

Cross-lingual word embeddings can be used directly as features in NLP models. Such models are then defined for several languages, and can be used to facilitate *cross-lingual transfer*. In other words, the main idea is to train a model on data from one language and then to apply it to another relying on shared cross-lingual features. Extrinsic evaluation on such downstream tasks is often preferred, as it directly allows to evaluate the usefulness of the cross-lingual word embedding model for the respective task. We briefly describe the cross-lingual tasks that people have used to evaluate cross-lingual word embeddings.

Document classification   Document classification is the task of classifying documents with respect to topic, sentiment, relevance, etc. The task is commonly used following the setup of (Klementiev et al., 2012): it uses the RCV2 Reuters multilingual corpus.[1] A document classifier is trained to predict topics on the document representations derived from word embeddings in the source language and then tested on the documents of the target language. A neural network model is trained to classify a given document in a language s in one of the pre-defined semantic classes. The neural network takes as input the word-embeddings $x_{i,j}^s$ of words $w_i, \ldots w_j$ which it

---

[1]http://trec.nist.gov/data/reuters/reuters.html

uses as features for classification. Once the neural network is trained for language s, it can be used to classify documents in another language t by simply using word embeddings in that language. If the embeddings are of high semantic quality that can be generalizable across languages, then the same network should give high accuracy of classification in both the languages. This task was originally introduced for English and German and then was extended to French, Swedish, and Chinese (Upadhyay et al., 2016) and has been shown to capture the semantic content of cross-lingual word embedddings.

Dependency parsing   Dependency parsing is the task that constructs the grammatical structure of a sentence, establishing typed relationships between "head" words and words which modify those heads. In a cross-lingual setting (Täckström et al., 2012) proposed a parser transfer model that employed cross-lingual similarity measures based on cross-lingual Brown clusters. When relying on cross-lingual word embeddings, similar to cross-lingual document classification, a dependency parsing model is trained using the embeddings for a source language and is then evaluated on a target language. In the setup of Guo et al. (2015),[2] a transition-based dependency parser is trained using word embeddings for language s and then the trained model is tested on language t by using word embeddings of that language.

POS tagging   POS tagging, the task of assigning parts-of-speech to words, is usually evaluated using the Universal Dependencies treebanks (Nivre et al., 2016) as these are annotated with the same universal tag set. Zhang et al. (2016b) furthermore map proper nouns to nouns and symbol makers (e.g., "-", "/") and interjections to an X tag as it is hard and unnecessary to disambiguate them in a low-resource setting. Fang and Cohn (2017) use data from the CoNLL-X datasets of European languages (Buchholz and Marsi, 2006), from CoNLL 2003[3] and from Das and Petrov (2011), the latter of which is also used by Gouws and Søgaard (2015).

Named entity recognition (NER)   NER is the task of tagging entities with their appropriate type in a text. Zou et al. (2013) perform NER experiments for English and Chinese on OntoNotes (Hovy et al., 2006), while Murthy et al. (2016) use English data from CoNLL 2003 (Tjong Kim Sang and De Meulder, 2003) and Spanish and Dutch data from CoNLL 2002 (Tjong Kim Sang and De Meulder, 2002).

Super-sense tagging   Super-sense tagging is the task that involves annotating each significant entity in a text (e.g., nouns, verbs, adjectives and adverbs) within a general semantic taxonomy defined by the WordNet lexicographer classes (called super-senses). The cross-lingual variant of the task is used by Gouws and Søgaard (2015) for evaluating their embeddings. They use the English data from SemCor[4] and publicly available Danish data.[5]

---

[2]https://github.com/jiangfeng1124/acl15-clnndep
[3]http://www.cnts.ua.ac.be/conll2003/ner/
[4]http://web.eecs.umich.edu/~mihalcea/downloads.html#semcor
[5]https://github.com/coastalcph/noda2015_sst

Semantic parsing   Semantic parsing is the task of automatically identifying semantically salient targets in the text. Frame-semantic parsing, in particular, disambiguates the targets by assigning a sense (frame) to them, identifies their arguments, and labels the arguments with appropriate roles. Johannsen et al. (2015) create a frame-semantic parsing corpus that covers five topics, two domains (Wikipedia and Twitter), and nine languages and use it to evaluate cross-lingual word embeddings.

Discourse parsing   Discourse parsing is the task of segmenting text into elementary discourse units (mostly clauses), which are then recursively connected via discourse relations to form complex discourse units. The segmentation is usually done according to Rhetorical Structure Theory (RST) (Mann and Thompson, 1988). Braud et al. (2017a,b) perform experiments using a diverse range of RST discourse treebanks for English, Portuguese, Spanish, German, Dutch, and Basque.

Dialog state tracking (DST)   DST is the component in task-oriented dialogue statistical systems that keeps track of the belief state, that is, the system's internal distribution over the possible states of the dialogue. A recent state-of-the-art DST model of Mrkšić et al. (2017) is based exclusively on word embeddings fed into the model as its input. This property of the model enables a straightforward adaptation to cross-lingual settings by simply replacing input monolingual word embeddings with cross-lingual word embeddings. Still an under-explored task, we believe that DST serves as a useful proxy task which shows the capability of induced word embeddings to support more complex language understanding tasks. Mrkšić et al. (2017) use DST for evaluating cross-lingual word embeddings on the Multilingual WOZ 2.0 dataset (Wen et al., 2017) available in English, German, and Italian. Their results suggest that cross-lingual word embeddings boost the construction of dialog state trackers in German and Italian even without any German and Italian training data, as the model is able to also exploit English training data through the embedding space. Further, a multilingual DST model which uses training data from all three languages combined with a multilingual word embedding space improves tracking performance in all three languages.

Entity linking or wikification   Entity linking or wikification is another task tackled using cross-lingual word embeddings (Tsai and Roth, 2016). The purpose of the task is to ground mentions written in non-English documents to entries in the English Wikipedia, facilitating the exploration and understanding of foreign texts without full-fledged translation systems (Ji et al., 2015). Such wikifiers, i.e., entity linkers are a valuable component of several NLP and IR tasks across different domains (Cheng and Roth, 2013, Mihalcea and Csomai, 2007).

Sentiment analysis   Sentiment analysis is the task of determining the sentiment polarity (e.g., positive and negative) of a text. Mogadala and Rettinger (2016) evaluate their embeddings on the multilingual Amazon product review dataset of Prettenhofer and Stein (2010).

Machine translation   Machine translation is used to translate entire texts in other languages. This is in contrast to bilingual dictionary induction, which focuses on the translation of individual words. Zou et al. (2013) used phrase-based machine translation to evaluate their embeddings. Cross-lingual word embeddings are incorporated in the phrase-based MT system by adding them as a feature to bilingual phrase-pairs. For each phrase, its word embeddings are averaged to obtain a feature vector. Cross-lingual word embeddings have also been shown to be helpful in the low-resource MT scenario (Gu et al., 2018a,b). Recently, several methods to perform machine translation without any parallel training data have been proposed (Artetxe et al., 2018c,d, Lample et al., 2018a,b, Yang et al., 2018). Such methods are particularly appealing for the translation of low-resource languages, where parallel data is scarce. While supervised neural machine translation (NMT) models *implicitly* learn a cross-lingual embedding space, current unsupervised NMT models *explicitly* use pretrained cross-lingual word embeddings. Specifically, cross-lingual word embeddings are learned using one of the unsupervised methods described in Chapter 9. These are then used to initialize the word representations of an unsupervised NMT model. While work on unsupervised MT is still in its infancy, recent methods suggest that cross-lingual word embeddings will play an important role. This opens up many exciting applications, such as bootstrapping NMT models for truly low-resource languages.

Word alignment prediction   For word alignment prediction, each word in a given source language sentence is aligned with the most similar target language word from the target language sentence. If a source language word is out of vocabulary, it is not aligned with anything, whereas target language out-of-vocabulary words are given a default minimum similarity score, and never aligned to any candidate source language word in practice (Levy et al., 2017). The inverse of the alignment error rate (1-AER) (Koehn, 2009) is typically used to measure performance, where higher scores mean better alignments. Levy et al. (2017) use alignment data from Hansards[6] and from four other sources (Graça et al., 2008, Holmqvist and Ahrenberg, 2011, Lambert et al., 2005, Mihalcea and Pedersen, 2003).

Bilingual dictionary induction   After the shared cross-lingual word embedding space is induced, given a list of N source language words $x_{u,1}, \ldots, x_{u,N}$, the task is to find a target language word t for each *query word* x_u relying on the representations in the space. Bilingual dictionary induction is appealing as an evaluation task, as high-quality, freely available, wide-coverage manually constructed dictionaries are still rare, especially for non-European languages. The task also provides initial intrinsic evidence on the quality of the shared space. Upadhyay et al. (2016) obtain evaluation sets for the task across 26 languages from the Open Multilingual WordNet (Bond and Foster, 2013), while Levy et al. (2017) obtain bilingual dictionaries from Wiktionary for Arabic, Finnish, Hebrew, Hungarian, and Turkish. More recently, Wijaya et al. (2017) build evaluation data for 28 language pairs (where English is always the target language) by semi-automatically translating all Wikipedia words with frequency above 100. Current evaluation

---

[6]https://www.isi.edu/natural-language/download/hansard/

datasets mostly focus on highly frequent words for evaluation of bilingual dictionary induction. Such an evaluation that focus on the head of the word stream often fails to generalize to the tail end where the infrequent word exists. Thus, a new dataset that focuses on rare words have been introduced by Braune et al. (2018) that contains words from both the general and medical domain for English-German language pair.

Information retrieval Word embeddings in general and cross-lingual word embeddings in specific have naturally found application beyond core NLP applications. They also offer support to Information Retrieval tasks (IR) (Mitra and Craswell, 2017, Zamani and Croft, 2016, inter alia) serving as useful features which can link semantics of the query to semantics of the target document collection, even when query terms are not explicitly mentioned in the relevant documents (e.g., the query can talk about *cars* while a relevant document may contain a near-synonym *automobile*). A shared cross-lingual word embedding space provides means to more general cross-lingual and multilingual IR models without any substantial change in the algorithmic design of the retrieval process (Vulić and Moens, 2015). Semantic similarity between query and document representations, obtained through the composition process as in the document classification task, is computed in the shared space, irrespective of their actual languages: the similarity score may be used as a measure of document relevance to the information need formulated in the issued query. Cross-lingual word embeddings are particularly useful for unsupervised cross-lingual IR (Litschko et al., 2018).

○ **Open Problem** How strong is the correlation between intrinsic and extrinsic tasks in cross-lingual NLP?

○ **Open Problem** Do different classes of word embedding methods support different classes of downstream tasks? Are word embeddings tuned for, e.g., bilingual lexicon induction, equally good in dependency parsing and in language understanding?

10.3 MULTI-MODAL AND COGNITIVE APPROACHES TO EVALUATION

Evaluation of monolingual word embeddings is a controversial topic. Monolingual word embeddings are useful downstream (Turian et al., 2010), but in order to argue that one set of embeddings is better than another, we would like a robust evaluation metric. Metrics have been proposed based on co-occurrences (perplexity or word error rate), based on ability to discriminate between contexts (e.g., topic classification), and based on lexical semantics (predicting links in lexical knowledge bases). Søgaard (2016) argues that such metrics are not valid, because co-occurrences, contexts, and lexical knowledge bases are also used to induce word embeddings, and that downstream evaluation is the best way to evaluate word embeddings. The only task-independent evaluation of embeddings that is reasonable, he claims, is to evaluate word embeddings by how well they predict behavioral observations, e.g., gaze or fMRI data.

For cross-lingual word embeddings, it is easier to come up with valid metrics, e.g., $P@k$,[7] in word alignment and bilingual dictionary induction. Note that these metrics only evaluate cross-lingual neighbors, not whether monolingual distances between words reflect synonymy relations. In other words, a random pairing of translation equivalents in vector space would score perfect precision in bilingual dictionary induction tasks. In addition, if we intend to evaluate the ability of cross-lingual word embeddings to allow for generalizations *within* languages, we inherit the problem of finding valid metrics from monolingual word representation learning.

---

[7]Precision at k is the average fraction of the top-k predictions of the model that are true translation equivalents.

CHAPTER 11

Useful Data and Software

A noteworthy tendency in NLP research is to ensure replicability of conducted research and shorten the time needed to enter a new domain of research by providing more and more directly usable code in readily accessible online repositories. In what follows, we provide a (non-exhaustive) list of links to online material that can provide hands-on support to NLP practitioners entering this vibrant field.

11.1 MONOLINGUAL RESOURCES

As some cross-lingual word embedding models leverage monolingual corpora and/or pre-trained monolingual word embeddings, it is also useful to point at some direct sources of monolingual data frequently used in NLP research. A typical starting point are Wikipedia corpora provided in multiple languages, such as the ones found in the Polyglot Wikipedia corpus (Al-Rfou et al., 2013): it contains preprocessed and tokenized Wikipedias (in the one-sentence-per-line plain text format) in 40 languages. The data is available here:

```
https://sites.google.com/site/rmyeid/projects/polyglot
```

Full Wikipedias in 23 languages provided in the XML format are also available from the Linguatools website:

```
http://linguatools.org/tools/corpora/wikipedia-monolingual-corpora/
```

Besides Wikipedia, continuing initiatives on collecting web-sized corpora have compiled large corpora in multiple languages through language-specific web crawling (Baroni et al., 2009, Benko, 2014, Ljubešić and Klubička, 2014, Sharoff, 2006). There is no standardized repository for all such corpora and they are not available for medium-sized and minor languages, but we point to several useful online repositories:

```
http://wacky.sslmit.unibo.it/doku.php?id=corpora
http://ucts.uniba.sk/aranea_about/
http://corpus.leeds.ac.uk/internet.html
https://www.clarin.si/repository/xmlui/
```

A starting point for mapping-based approaches to cross-lingual embedding learning are pre-trained monolingual word embeddings in different languages. Probably the largest collection of such pre-trained embeddings are FASTTEXT embeddings trained on Wikipedia data for 294 languages (Bojanowski et al., 2017):

```
https://fasttext.cc/docs/en/pretrained-vectors.html
```

11.2   CROSS-LINGUAL DATA

A crucial aspect of cross-lingual word embedding learning concerns the actual source of bilingual supervision: dictionaries, lexical databases, and parallel or comparable bilingual data. Resources for word-level supervision can be found in a multitude of bilingual lexicons available online. Some initiatives such as BabelNet (Ehrmann et al., 2014, Navigli and Ponzetto, 2012) and PanLex (Baldwin et al., 2010, Kamholz et al., 2014) have compiled lexicons for many languages in a single resource (e.g., the latest BabelNet version 4.0 covers 284 languages).

```
https://babelnet.org/
https://panlex.org/
```

Another useful source of cross-lingual lexical knowledge used in prior work concerns on-line translation services such as Google Translate or Bing Microsoft Translator, as well as a variety of smaller bilingual lexicons for particular language pairs (e.g., dict.cc for English-German). A large collection of parallel corpora in different domains (e.g., newswire, parliamentary proceedings, healthcare, legal texts) and for different language pairs is actively maintained as part of the OPUS initiative (Tiedemann, 2012):

```
http://opus.nlpl.eu/
```

Other similar parallel corpora are scattered around the Web, so the OPUS website is perhaps the best starting point. Newswire document-aligned corpora can be crawled from bilingual news websites such as BBC or Reuters, but the most used document-aligned corpus is Wikipedia where articles in different languages are aligned through interlingual Wikipedia links. The Linguatools website provide document-aligned comparable corpora for 253 language pairs in total, covering 23 languages:

```
http://linguatools.org/tools/corpora/wikipedia-comparable-corpora/
```

11.3   CROSS-LINGUAL WORD EMBEDDING MODELS

A majority of prominent cross-lingual embedding models are available online. Due to high storage demands of word embeddings in general, which increase even more when moving from monolingual settings (single languages) to bilingual settings (language pairs), the available material is mostly directly usable code that can be applied on monolingual and cross-lingual data from previous sections. We provide links to some of the well-known models representative of different types according to the model typology from Chapter 3. The implementation of the basic bilingual mapping-based approach of Mikolov et al. (2013b), also used in follow-up work (Dinu et al., 2015, Vulić and Korhonen, 2016), is extremely easy and can be found in several software packages:

```
http://clic.cimec.unitn.it/~georgiana.dinu/down/
https://github.com/artetxem/vecmap
```

Further extensions to the basic mapping-based framework have been proposed and implemented. A variant of the model which induces a multilingual embedding space has been proposed by Smith et al. (2017). The provided API has been tested on monolingual FASTTEXT embeddings, but is equally applicable to any other set of pre-trained monolingual embeddings. The main practical contribution of that work is concerned with providing bilingual English-to-target-language dictionaries and pre-trained matrices that can be used to perform the mapping between English and 78 other (target) languages. A multilingual space is induced by treating English as a hub language. The software is available at:

```
https://github.com/Babylonpartners/fastText_multilingual
```

The implementation of a bootstrapping mapping-based approach of Artetxe et al. which relies on weak supervision (e.g., shared words or numerals) (Artetxe et al., 2017) is available at:

```
https://github.com/artetxem/vecmap
```

The same software package also contains of a fully unsupervised cross-lingual embedding model (Artetxe et al., 2018b). Ruder et al. (2018) have extended the work of Artetxe et al. to allow an optimal 1:1 mapping, which can be found at:

```
https://github.com/sebastianruder/latent-variable-vecmap
```

Another unsupervised mapping-based model from Conneau et al. (2018) is also available online, along with translation dictionaries compiled automatically from Google Translate:

```
https://github.com/facebookresearch/MUSE
```

Besides mapping-based approaches, other models which learn on the basis of word-level alignment are also available online. The implementations of the CCA-based approach of Faruqui and Dyer (2014), Deep CCA-based approach of Lu et al. (2015), and Deep Partial CCA-based approach of Rotman et al. (2018) can be obtained following the respective links:

```
https://github.com/mfaruqui/crosslingual-cca
https://github.com/msamribeiro/deep-cca
https://github.com/rotmanguy/DPCCA
```

The BiSkip model of Luong et al. (2015) is available at:

```
https://github.com/lmthang/bivec
```

An implementation of a similar model of Duong et al. (2016), which relies on bilingual dictionaries instead of word alignments from parallel data, is available at:

```
https://github.com/longdt219/XlingualEmb
```

An implementation of the BilBOWA model (Gouws et al., 2015), an instance of a joint approach that learns from sentence-level alignment, is available at:

```
https://github.com/gouwsmeister/bilbowa
```

Another model that learns from sentence-level alignments is the BiCVM model (Hermann and Blunsom, 2014), available online at:

```
https://github.com/karlmoritz/bicvm
```

An implementation of a representative pseudo-mixing approach from Vulić and Moens (2016) which learns on the basis of document-level alignment is also available online in the following repository:

```
https://github.com/cambridgeltl/bwesg
```

Finally, reimplementations of several models can be found in a single repository (Berard et al., 2016):

```
https://github.com/eske/multivec
```

11.4   EVALUATION AND APPLICATION

Two main ways to evaluate and use word embeddings, as discussed in Chapter 10 are: (1) to compute (cross-lingual) semantic similarity by applying a similarity measure (e.g., cosine or more sophisticated methods such as cross-domain domain local similarity scaling (Conneau et al., 2018)) on the embeddings and (2) to use the embeddings as feature vectors that support cross-lingual downstream tasks such as cross-lingual and multilingual dependency parsing, document classification, and machine translation.

The most common evaluations based on similarity scores are cross-lingual word similarity and bilingual lexicon extraction. The resources for the former are very scarce: the only benchmark is the dataset generated for a SemEval 2017 task (Camacho-Collados et al., 2017). The dataset contains word pairs scored for similarity for all language pairs among the set of five languages: English, German, Italian, Spanish, and Farsi

```
http://alt.qcri.org/semeval2017/task2/
```

Evaluation data for bilingual lexicon induction are more abundant and can be sampled from previously mentioned cross-lingual lexical resources (e.g., BabelNet, PanLex) and tools (e.g., Google Translate). Note that the data automatically constructed from Google Translate typically requires an additional manual verification step, especially for more distant language pairs. Current test data for language pairs such as English-Finnish, often used in the most recent work (Artetxe et al., 2018b, Conneau et al., 2018) are of insufficient quality and higher-quality test sets are sought. Another gap in the current evaluation lies in the fact that most evaluation data contains English as one of the languages, and test sets for other language pairs are still scarce and there are no standardized benchmarks.

Several comparative empirical studies have created repositories that facilitate the evaluation of cross-lingual word embeddings in downstream tasks of cross-lingual dependency parsing and document classification (Ammar et al., 2016b, Upadhyay et al., 2016):

```
http://128.2.220.95/multilingual/
https://github.com/shyamupa/biling-survey
```

Dependency parsing and POS tagging are perhaps the most popular downstream evaluation tasks due to the availability of high-quality cross-linguistically consistent annotations provided in the Universal Dependencies project:

```
http://universaldependencies.org/
```

Implementations of unsupervised machine translation systems based on cross-lingual embeddings (Artetxe et al., 2018d, Lample et al., 2018a) are also available online:

```
https://github.com/artetxem/undreamt
https://github.com/artetxem/monoses
https://github.com/facebookresearch/UnsupervisedMT
https://github.com/OpenNMT/OpenNMT
```

In summary, constructing comprehensive and high-quality evaluation data, especially for downstream evaluation of text representations, is still one of the main challenges in modern NLP, as such evaluation resources are typically available only for a small subset of major languages. This is even more exacerbated in cross-lingual scenarios where such resources are required for a wide variety of language pairs. The lack of cross-lingual evaluation data for language pairs across different language families and types still limits our ability to fully generalize our current NLP methodology toward true language universals, and hinders the construction of truly language pair independent robust representation architectures.

CHAPTER 12

General Challenges and Future Directions

This book has focused on providing an overview of cross-lingual word embedding models. It has introduced standardized notation and a typology that demonstrated the similarity of many of these models. It provided proofs that connect different word-level embedding models and has described ways to evaluate cross-lingual word embeddings, as well as how to extend them to the multilingual setting. Below we outline existing challenges and possible future research directions.

Subword-level information In morphologically rich languages, words can have complex internal structures, and some word forms can be rare. For such languages, it makes sense to compose representations from representations of lemmas and morphemes. Neural network models increasingly leverage subword-level information (Lample et al., 2016, Sennrich et al., 2016) and character-based input has been found useful for sharing knowledge in multilingual scenarios (Gillick et al., 2016, Ling et al., 2016). Subword-level information has also been used for learning word representations (Bhatia et al., 2016, Ling et al., 2015) but has so far not been incorporated in learning cross-lingual word representations.

○ **Open Problem** How do we best align vector spaces for languages with very different morphologies, i.e., where the information encoded in a single word in one language may require phrases in the other language?

Multi-word expressions Just like words can be too coarse units for representation learning in morphologically rich languages, words also combine in non-compositional ways to form multi-word expressions such as *ad hoc* or *kick the bucket*, the meaning of which cannot be derived from standard representations of their constituents. Dealing with multi-word expressions remains a challenge for monolingual applications and has only received scarce attention in the cross-lingual setting.

○ **Open Problem** Can we use current techniques to also align multi-word expressions across languages?

Function words Models for learning cross-linguistic representations share weaknesses with other vector space models of language: while they are very good at modeling the conceptual aspect of meaning evaluated in word similarity tasks, they fail to properly model the functional aspect of meaning, e.g., to distinguish whether one remarks "Give me *a* pencil" or "Give me *that* pencil." Modeling the functional aspect of language is of particular importance in scenarios such as dialogue, where the pragmatics of language must be taken into account.

Polysemy   While conflating multiple senses of a word is already problematic for learning monolingual word representations, this issue is amplified in a cross-lingual word embedding space: if polysemy leads to m bad word embeddings in the source language, and n bad word embeddings in the target language, we can derive $\mathcal{O}(n \times m)$ false nearest neighbors from our cross-lingual word embeddings. While recent work on learning cross-lingual multi-sense embeddings (Li and Jurafsky, 2015) is extremely interesting, it is still an open question whether modern NLP models can infer from context, what they need in order to resolve lexical ambiguities.

○ **Open Problem**   Do we need sense-level representations in cross-lingual NLP?

Embeddings for specialized domains   There are many domains, for which cross-lingual applications would be particularly useful, such as bioinformatics or social media. However, parallel data is scarce in many such domains as well as for low-resource languages. Creating robust cross-lingual word representations with as few parallel examples as possible is thus an important research avenue. An important related direction is to leverage comparable corpora, which are often more plentiful and incorporate other signals, such as from multi-modal contexts.

Feasibility   Learning a general shared vector space for words that reliably captures inter-language and intra-language relations may seem slightly optimistic. Languages are very different, and it is not clear if there is even a definition of *words* that make words commensurable across languages. Note that while this is related to whether it is possible to translate between the world's languages in the first place, the possibility of translation (at document level) does not necessarily entail that it is possible to device embeddings such that translation equivalents in two languages end up as nearest neighbors, or vice versa. Another bottleneck may be the computational complexity of finding embeddings that obey all our inter-lingual and intra-lingual constraints, say, for example, translation equivalents and synonymy. Currently, many approaches to cross-lingual word embeddings, as shown in this survey, minimize a loss that penalizes models for violating such constraints, but there is no guarantee that the final model satisfies all constraints. Checking whether all such constraints are satisfied in a given model is trivially done in time linear in the number of constraints, but finding out whether such a model exists is much harder. While the problem's decidability follows from the decidability of two-variable first order logic with equivalence/symmetry closure, determining whether such a graph exists is in fact NP-hard (Eades and Whitesides, 1995).

Nonlinear mapping   Mapping-based approaches assume that a linear transformation can project the embedding space of one language into the space of a target language. While Mikolov et al. (2013b) and Conneau et al. (2018) both find that a linear transformation outperforms nonlinear transformation learned via a feedforward neural network, assuming a linear transformation between two languages is overly simplistic and ignores important language-specific differences. Nakashole and Flauger (2018) lend further credibility to this intuition by learning neighborhood-specific linear transformations and showing that these vary across the monolingual word embedding space. However, to the best of our knowledge, there has not been any model yet that leveraged this intuition to construct a more effective mapping model.

○ **Open Problem**   How can we robustly learn nonlinear maps between vector spaces?

Robust unsupervised approaches   In Chapter 9, we discussed approaches relying only on small seed lexicons (Artetxe et al., 2017, Zhang et al., 2016a), as well as completely unsupervised approaches that seek to match source and target distributions based on adversarial learning (Conneau et al., 2018, Zhang et al., 2017a,b). Unsupervised methods rely on the assumption that monolingual word embedding spaces are approximately isomorphic, which is generally not the case (Søgaard et al., 2018), and many of these methods are unstable or unsuccessful when confronted with distant language pairs. In simple terms, although thought-provoking and attractive in theory, such unsupervised methods seem to fail when languages are distant, and we believe it is fair to say that robust unsupervised induction of bilingual lexicons for distant language pairs remains an open problem.

Bibliography

Oliver Adams, Adam Makarucha, Graham Neubig, Steven Bird, and Trevor Cohn. 2017. Cross-lingual word embeddings for low-resource language modeling. In *Proc. of the 15th Conference of the European Chapter of the Association for Computational Linguistics: (Volume 1, Long Papers)*, pages 937–947. DOI: 10.18653/v1/e17-1088 16, 19, 41

Rami Al-Rfou, Bryan Perozzi, and Steven Skiena. 2013. Polyglot: Distributed word representations for multilingual NLP. In *Proc. of the 17th Conference on Computational Natural Language Learning*, pages 183–192. 83

Jean Alaux, Edouard Grave, Marco Cuturi, and Armand Joulin. 2018. Unsupervised hyper-alignment for multilingual word embeddings. In *Proc. of the 7th International Conference on Learning Representations*. 16

David Alvarez-Melis and Tommi S. Jaakkola. 2018. Gromov-Wasserstein alignment of word embedding spaces. In *Proc. of the Conference on Empirical Methods in Natural Language Processing*, pages 1881–1890. 16, 38

Waleed Ammar, George Mulcaire, Miguel Ballesteros, Chris Dyer, and Noah A. Smith. 2016a. Many languages, one parser. *Transactions of the Association for Computational Linguistics*, 4:431–444. DOI: 10.1162/tacl_a_00109 1, 18, 19, 21, 32

Waleed Ammar, George Mulcaire, Yulia Tsvetkov, Guillaume Lample, Chris Dyer, and Noah A. Smith. 2016b. Massively multilingual word embeddings. *CoRR*, abs/1602.01925. 16, 37, 41, 60, 64, 76, 87

Ghinatsu Aone and Douglas McKee. 1993. A language-independent anaphora resolution system for understanding multilingual texts. In *Proc. of the 31st Annual Meeting of the Association for Computational Linguistics*, pages 156–163. DOI: 10.3115/981574.981595 21

Martín Arjovsky, Soumith Chintala, and Léon Bottou. 2017. Wasserstein generative adversarial networks. In *Proc. of the 34th International Conference on Machine Learning*, pages 214–223. 69, 70

Mikel Artetxe, Gorka Labaka, and Eneko Agirre. 2016. Learning principled bilingual mappings of word embeddings while preserving monolingual invariance. In *Proc. of the Conference on Empirical Methods in Natural Language Processing*, pages 2289–2294. DOI: 10.18653/v1/d16-1250 16, 18, 36, 37

Mikel Artetxe, Gorka Labaka, and Eneko Agirre. 2017. Learning bilingual word embeddings with (almost) no bilingual data. In *Proc. of the 55th Annual Meeting of the Association for Computational Linguistics (Volume 1: Long Papers)*, pages 451–462. DOI: 10.18653/v1/p17-1042 16, 18, 26, 38, 39, 67, 85, 91

Mikel Artetxe, Gorka Labaka, and Eneko Agirre. 2018a. Generalizing and improving bilingual word embedding mappings with a multi-step framework of linear transformations. In *Proc. of the 32nd AAAI Conference on Artificial Intelligence*, pages 5012–5019. 16, 20, 37, 73

Mikel Artetxe, Gorka Labaka, and Eneko Agirre. 2018b. A robust self-learning method for fully unsupervised cross-lingual mappings of word embeddings. In *Proc. of the 56th Annual Meeting of the Association for Computational Linguistics (Volume 1: Long Papers)*, pages 789–798. 16, 26, 38, 39, 67, 68, 69, 72, 73, 74, 85, 87

Mikel Artetxe, Gorka Labaka, and Eneko Agirre. 2018c. Unsupervised statistical machine translation. In *Proc. of the Conference on Empirical Methods in Natural Language Processing*, pages 3632–3642. 79

Mikel Artetxe, Gorka Labaka, Eneko Agirre, and Kyunghyun Cho. 2018d. Unsupervised neural machine translation. In *Proc. of the 6th International Conference on Learning Representations*. 4, 79, 87

Amir Bakarov, Roman Suvorov, and Ilya Sochenkov. 2018. The limitations of cross-language word embeddings evaluation. In *Proc. of the 7th Joint Conference on Lexical and Computational Semantics*, pages 94–100. DOI: 10.18653/v1/s18-2010 76

Timothy Baldwin, Jonathan Pool, and Susan Colowick. 2010. PanLex and LEXTRACT: Translating all words of all languages of the world. In *Proc. of the 23rd International Conference on Computational Linguistics (Demo Papers)*, pages 37–40. 84

Antonio Valerio Miceli Barone. 2016. Towards cross-lingual distributed representations without parallel text trained with adversarial autoencoders. In *Proc. of the 1st Workshop on Representation Learning for NLP*, pages 121–126. DOI: 10.18653/v1/w16-1614 68, 72

Marco Baroni, Silvia Bernardini, Adriano Ferraresi, and Eros Zanchetta. 2009. The WaCky wide web: A collection of very large linguistically processed web-crawled corpora. *Language Resources and Evaluation*, 43(3):209–226. DOI: 10.1007/s10579-009-9081-4 83

Maria Barrett, Frank Keller, and Anders Søgaaard. 2016. Cross-lingual transfer of correlations between parts of speech and gaze features. In *Proc. of the 26th International Conference on Computational Linguistics (Technical Papers)*, pages 1330–1339. 14, 47

Yoshua Bengio, Réjean Ducharme, Pascal Vincent, and Christian Janvin. 2003. A neural probabilistic language model. *Journal of Machine Learning Research*, 3:1137–1155. DOI: 10.1007/10985687_6 23, 42

Vladimír Benko. 2014. Aranea: Yet another family of (comparable) Web corpora. In *Proc. of the 17th International Conference on Text, Speech and Dialogue*, pages 247–254. DOI: 10.1007/978-3-319-10816-2_31 83

Alexandre Berard, Christophe Servan, Olivier Pietquin, and Laurent Besacier. 2016. MultiVec: A multilingual and multilevel representation learning toolkit for NLP. In *Proc. of the 10th International Conference on Language Resources and Evaluation*, pages 4188–4192. 86

Shane Bergsma and Benjamin Van Durme. 2011. Learning bilingual lexicons using the visual similarity of labeled Web images. In *Proc. of the 22nd International Joint Conference on Artificial Intelligence*, pages 1764–1769. DOI: 10.5591/978-1-57735-516-8/IJCAI11-296 14, 19, 46

Paul J. Besl and Neil D. McKay. 1992. A method for registration of 3D shapes. *IEEE Transactions on Pattern Analysis and Machine Intelligence*, 14(2):239–256. DOI: 10.1109/34.121791 70

Parminder Bhatia, Robert Guthrie, and Jacob Eisenstein. 2016. Morphological priors for probabilistic neural word embeddings. In *Proc. of the Conference on Empirical Methods in Natural Language Processing*, pages 490–500. DOI: 10.18653/v1/d16-1047 89

David M. Blei, Andrew Y. Ng, and Michael I. Jordan. 2003. Latent Dirichlet allocation. *Journal of Machine Learning Research*, 3:993–1022. 31

Piotr Bojanowski, Edouard Grave, Armand Joulin, and Tomas Mikolov. 2017. Enriching word vectors with subword information. *Transactions of the Association for Computational Linguistics*, 5:135–146. DOI: 10.1162/tacl_a_00051 12, 60, 72, 84

Francis Bond and Ryan Foster. 2013. Linking and extending an Open Multilingual WordNet. In *Proc. of the 51st Annual Meeting of the Association for Computational Linguistics (Volume 1: Long Papers)*, pages 1352–1362. 79

Jordan Boyd-Graber and David M. Blei. 2009. Multilingual topic models for unaligned text. In *Proc. of the 25th Conference on Uncertainty in Artificial Intelligence*, pages 75–82. 31

Jordan Boyd-Graber, Yuening Hu, and David Mimno. 2017. *Applications of Topic Models*, volume 11 of *Foundations and Trends in Information Retrieval*. DOI: 10.1561/1500000030 29

Jordan Boyd-Graber and Philip Resnik. 2010. Holistic sentiment analysis across languages: Multilingual supervised Latent Dirichlet Allocation. In *Proc. of the Conference on Empirical Methods in Natural Language Processing*, pages 45–55. 31

Chloé Braud, Maximin Coavoux, and Anders Søgaard. 2017a. Cross-lingual RST discourse parsing. In *Proc. of the 15th Conference of the European Chapter of the Association for Computational Linguistics: (Volume 1, Long Papers)*, pages 292–304. DOI: 10.18653/v1/e17-1028 78

Chloé Braud, Ophélie Lacroix, and Anders Søgaard. 2017b. Cross-lingual and cross-domain discourse segmentation of entire documents. In *Proc. of the 55th Annual Meeting of the Association for Computational Linguistics (Volume 2: Short Papers)*, pages 237–243. DOI: 10.18653/v1/p17-2037 78

Fabienne Braune, Viktor Hangya, Tobias Eder, and Alexander Fraser. 2018. Evaluating bilingual word embeddings on the long tail. In *Proc. of the Conference of the North American Chapter of the Association for Computational Linguistics: Human Language Technologies (Volume 2: Short Papers)*, pages 188–193. DOI: 10.18653/v1/n18-2030 80

Peter F. Brown, Stephen Della Pietra, Vincent J. Della Pietra, and Robert L. Mercer. 1993. The mathematics of statistical machine translation: Parameter estimation. *Computational Linguistics*, 19(2):263–311. 27, 28, 51

Peter F. Brown, Vincent J. Della Pietra, Peter V. de Souza, Jennifer C. Lai, and Robert L. Mercer. 1992. Class-based n-gram models of natural language. *Computational Linguistics*, 18(4):467–479. 23

Elia Bruni, Nam-Khanh Tran, and Marco Baroni. 2014. Multimodal distributional semantics. *Journal of Artificial Intelligence Research*, 49(2014):1–47. DOI: 10.1613/jair.4135 75

Sabine Buchholz and Erwin Marsi. 2006. CoNLL-X Shared task on multilingual dependency parsing. In *Proc. of the 10th Conference on Computational Natural Language Learning*, pages 149–164. DOI: 10.3115/1596276.1596305 77

Iacer Calixto, Qun Liu, and Nick Campbell. 2017. Sentence-level multilingual multi-modal embedding for natural language processing. In *Proc. of the 11th International Conference on Recent Advances in Natural Language Processing*, pages 139–148. DOI: 10.26615/978-954-452-049-6_020 14, 17, 18, 53

Jose Camacho-Collados, Mohammad Taher Pilehvar, Nigel Collier, and Roberto Navigli. 2017. SemEval-2017 Task 2: Multilingual and cross-lingual semantic word similarity. In *Proc. of the 11th International Workshop on Semantic Evaluation (SemEval-2017)*, pages 15–26. DOI: 10.18653/v1/s17-2002 75, 87

José Camacho-Collados, Mohammad Taher Pilehvar, and Roberto Navigli. 2015. A framework for the construction of monolingual and cross-lingual word similarity datasets. In *Proc. of the 53rd Annual Meeting of the Association for Computational Linguistics and the 7th International Joint Conference on Natural Language Processing (Volume 2: Short Papers)*, pages 1–7. DOI: 10.3115/v1/p15-2001 75

Giovanni Cavallanti, Nicolo Cesa-Bianchi, and Claudio Gentile. 2010. Linear algorithms for online multitask classification. *Journal of Machine Learning Research*, 11:2901–2934. 42

Sarath Chandar, Stanislas Lauly, Hugo Larochelle, Mitesh M. Khapra, Balaraman Ravindran, Vikas Raykar, and Amrita Saha. 2014. An autoencoder approach to learning bilingual word representations. In *Proc. of the 27th Annual Conference on Neural Information Processing Systems*, pages 1853–1861. 17, 18, 51, 64

Xilun Chen and Claire Cardie. 2018. Unsupervised multilingual word embeddings. In *Proc. of the Conference on Empirical Methods in Natural Language Processing*, pages 261–270. 16

Xiao Cheng and Dan Roth. 2013. Relational inference for wikification. In *Proc. of the Conference on Empirical Methods in Natural Language Processing*, pages 1787–1796. 78

Kenneth Ward Church and Patrick Hanks. 1990. Word association norms, mutual information, and lexicography. *Computational Linguistics*, 16(1):22–29. DOI: 10.3115/981623.981633 9

Ann Cocos and Chris Callison-Burch. 2017. The language of place: Semantic value from geospatial context. In *Proc. of the 15th Conference of the European Chapter of the Association for Computational Linguistics (Volume 2: Short Papers)*, pages 99–104. DOI: 10.18653/v1/e17-2016 14

Shay Cohen, Dipanjan Das, and Noah Smith. 2011. Unsupervised structure prediction with non-parallel multilingual guidance. In *Proc. of the Conference on Empirical Methods in Natural Language Processing*, pages 50–61. 21

Ronan Collobert and Jason Weston. 2008. A unified architecture for natural language processing: Deep neural networks with multitask learning. In *Proc. of the 25th International Conference on Machine Learning*, pages 160–167. DOI: 10.1145/1390156.1390177 9, 37, 41

Alexis Conneau, Guillaume Lample, Marc'Aurelio Ranzato, Ludovic Denoyer, and Hervé Jégou. 2018. Word translation without parallel data. In *Proc. of the 6th International Conference on Learning Representations*. 16, 26, 38, 39, 67, 68, 69, 71, 72, 73, 85, 86, 87, 90, 91

Jocelyn Coulmance, Jean-Marc Marty, Guillaume Wenzek, and Amine Benhalloum. 2015. Trans-gram, fast cross-lingual word-embeddings. In *Proc. of the Conference on Empirical Methods in Natural Language Processing*, pages 1109–1113. DOI: 10.18653/v1/d15-1131 17, 19, 51, 52, 64, 65

Sune Darkner, Martin Vester-Christensen, Rasmus Larsen, Claus Nielsen, and Rasmus Reinhold Paulsen. 2006. Automated 3D rigid registration of open 2D manifolds. In *Proc. of the Conference on Medical Image Computing and Computer Assisted Intervention (Workshop Track)*, pages 19–22. 70

Dipanjan Das and Slav Petrov. 2011. Unsupervised part-of-speech tagging with bilingual graph-based projections. In *Proc. of the 49th Annual Meeting of the Association for Computational Linguistics: Human Language Technologies*, pages 600–609. 77

Wim De Smet, Jie Tang, and Marie-Francine Moens. 2011. Knowledge transfer across multilingual corpora via latent topics. In *Proc. of the 15th Pacific-Asia Conference on Knowledge Discovery and Data Mining*, pages 549–560. DOI: 10.1007/978-3-642-20841-6_45 31, 32

Scott Deerwester, Susan T. Dumais, George W. Furnas, Thomas K. Landauer, and Richard Harshman. 1990. Indexing by latent semantic analysis. *Journal of the American Society for Information Science*, 41(6):391–407. DOI: 10.1002/(sici)1097-4571(199009)41:6<391::aid-asi1>3.0.co;2-9 9

Mathieu Dehouck and Pascal Denis. 2017. Delexicalized word embeddings for cross-lingual dependency parsing. In *Proc. of the 15th Conference of the European Chapter of the Association for Computational Linguistics (Volume 1: Long Papers)*, pages 241–250. DOI: 10.18653/v1/e17-1023 21

Arthur P. Dempster, Nan M. Laird, and Donald B. Rubin. 1977. Maximum likelihood from incomplete data via the EM algorithm. *Journal of the Royal Statistical Society*, 39(1):1–22. DOI: 10.1111/j.2517-6161.1977.tb01600.x 6

Georgiana Dinu, Angeliki Lazaridou, and Marco Baroni. 2015. Improving zero-shot learning by mitigating the hubness problem. In *Proc. of the 3rd International Conference on Learning Representations (Workshop Track)*. 16, 18, 36, 37, 39, 71, 85

Yerai Doval, Luis Espinosa-Anke Jose Camacho-Collados, and Steven Schockaert. 2018. Improving cross-lingual word embeddings by meeting in the middle. In *Proc. of the Conference on Empirical Methods in Natural Language Processing*, pages 294–304. 16, 62

Philipp Dufter, Mengjie Zhao, Martin Schmitt, Alexander Fraser, and Hinrich Schütze. 2018. Embedding learning through multilingual concept induction. In *Proc. of the 56th Annual Meeting of the Association for Computational Linguistics (Volume 1: Long Papers)*, pages 1520–1530. 17

Long Duong, Trevor Cohn, Steven Bird, and Paul Cook. 2015. Cross-lingual transfer for unsupervised dependency parsing without parallel data. In *Proc. of the 19th Conference on Computational Natural Language Learning*, pages 113–122. DOI: 10.18653/v1/k15-1012 19, 21, 47

Long Duong, Hiroshi Kanayama, Tengfei Ma, Steven Bird, and Trevor Cohn. 2016. Learning crosslingual word embeddings without bilingual corpora. In *Proc. of the Conference on Empirical Methods in Natural Language Processing*, pages 1285–1295. DOI: 10.18653/v1/d16-1136 16, 19, 41, 63, 86

Long Duong, Hiroshi Kanayama, Tengfei Ma, Steven Bird, and Trevor Cohn. 2017. Multilingual training of crosslingual word embeddings. In *Proc. of the 15th Conference of the European*

Chapter of the Association for Computational Linguistics (Volume 1: Long Papers), pages 894–904. DOI: 10.18653/v1/e17-1084 59, 62, 63

Chris Dyer, Victor Chahuneau, and Noah A. Smith. 2013. A simple, fast, and effective reparameterization of IBM Model 2. In *Proc. of the Conference of the North American Chapter of the Association for Computational Linguistics: Human Language Technologies*, pages 644–648. 29

Chris Dyer, Adam Lopez, Juri Ganitkevitch, Jonathan Weese, Ferhan Ture, Phil Blunsom, Hendra Setiawan, Vladimir Eidelman, and Philip Resnik. 2010. CDEC: A decoder, alignment, and learning framework for finite-state and context-free translation models. In *Proc. of the 48th Annual Meeting of the Association for Computational Linguistics: Human Language Technologies (System Demonstrations)*, pages 7–12. 29

Peter Eades and Sue Whitesides. 1995. Nearest neighbour graph realizability is NP-hard. In *Proc. of the 2nd Latin American Symposium on Theoretical Informatics*, pages 245–256. DOI: 10.1007/3-540-59175-3_93 90

Maud Ehrmann, Francesco Cecconi, Daniele Vannella, John Philip Mccrae, Philipp Cimiano, and Roberto Navigli. 2014. Representing multilingual data as linked data: The case of BabelNet 2.0. In *Proc. of the 9th International Conference on Language Resources and Evaluation*, pages 401–408. 84

Desmond Elliott and Ákos Kádár. 2017. Imagination improves multimodal translation. In *Proc. of the 8th International Joint Conference on Natural Language Processing (Volume 1: Long Papers)*, pages 130–141. 53

Esther Ezra, Micha Sharir, and Alon Efrat. 2006. On the ICP algorithm. In *Proc. of the 22nd ACM Symposium on Computational Geometry*, pages 95–104. DOI: 10.1145/1137856.1137873 70

Meng Fang and Trevor Cohn. 2017. Model transfer for tagging low-resource languages using a bilingual dictionary. In *Proc. of the 55th Annual Meeting of the Association for Computational Linguistics (Volume 2: Short Papers)*, pages 587–593. DOI: 10.18653/v1/p17-2093 77

Manaal Faruqui, Jesse Dodge, Sujay K. Jauhar, Chris Dyer, Eduard Hovy, and Noah A. Smith. 2015. Retrofitting word vectors to semantic lexicons. In *Proc. of the Conference of the North American Chapter of the Association for Computational Linguistics: Human Language Technologies*, pages 1606–1615. DOI: 10.3115/v1/n15-1184 40, 45

Manaal Faruqui and Chris Dyer. 2013. An information theoretic approach to bilingual word clustering. In *Proc. of the 51st Annual Meeting of the Association for Computational Linguistics (Volume 2: Short Papers)*, pages 777–783. 21, 23

Manaal Faruqui and Chris Dyer. 2014. Improving vector space word representations using multilingual correlation. In *Proc. of the 14th Conference of the European Chapter of the Association for Computational Linguistics*, pages 462–471. DOI: 10.3115/v1/e14-1049 14, 16, 18, 26, 36, 37, 53, 59, 85

Manaal Faruqui and Shankar Kumar. 2015. Multilingual open relation extraction using cross-lingual projection. In *Proc. of the Conference of the North American Chapter of the Association for Computational Linguistics: Human Language Technologies*, pages 1351–1356. DOI: 10.3115/v1/n15-1151 32

Manaal Faruqui, Yulia Tsvetkov, Pushpendre Rastogi, and Chris Dyer. 2016. Problems with evaluation of word embeddings using word similarity tasks. In *Proc. of the 1st Workshop on Evaluating Vector-Space Representations for NLP*, pages 30–35. DOI: 10.18653/v1/w16-2506 76

Lev Finkelstein, Evgeniy Gabrilovich, Yossi Matias, Ehud Rivlin, Zach Solan, Gadi Wolfman, and Eytan Ruppin. 2002. Placing search in context: The concept revisited. *ACM Transactions on Information Systems*, 20(1):116–131. DOI: 10.1145/503104.503110 75

Kosuke Fukumasu, Koji Eguchi, and Eric P. Xing. 2012. Symmetric correspondence topic models for multilingual text analysis. In *Proc. of the 26th Annual Conference on Neural Information Processing Systems*, pages 1295–1303. 31

Pascale Fung and Lo Yuen Yee. 1998. An IR approach for translating new words from nonparallel, comparable texts. In *Proc. of the 36th Annual Meeting of the Association for Computational Linguistics and 17th International Conference on Computational Linguistics, (Volume 1)*, pages 414–420. DOI: 10.3115/980451.980916 25

Evgeniy Gabrilovich and Shaul Markovitch. 2006. Overcoming the brittleness bottleneck using Wikipedia: Enhancing text categorization with encyclopedic knowledge. In *Proc. of the 21st AAAI Conference on Artificial Intelligence*, pages 1301–1306. 32

Éric Gaussier, Jean-Michel Renders, Irina Matveeva, Cyril Goutte, and Hervé Déjean. 2004. A geometric view on bilingual lexicon extraction from comparable corpora. In *Proc. of the 42nd Annual Meeting of the Association for Computational Linguistics: Main Volume*, pages 526–533. DOI: 10.3115/1218955.1219022 25, 26

Spandana Gella, Rico Sennrich, Frank Keller, and Mirella Lapata. 2017. Image pivoting for learning multilingual multimodal representations. In *Proc. of the Conference on Empirical Methods in Natural Language Processing*, pages 2839–2845. DOI: 10.18653/v1/d17-1303 14, 17, 18, 53

Daniela Gerz, Ivan Vulić, Felix Hill, Roi Reichart, and Anna Korhonen. 2016. SimVerb-3500: A large-scale evaluation set of verb similarity. In *Proc. of the Conference on Empirical Methods in Natural Language Processing*, pages 2173–2182. DOI: 10.18653/v1/d16-1235 75

Dan Gillick, Cliff Brunk, Oriol Vinyals, and Amarnag Subramanya. 2016. Multilingual language processing from bytes. In *Proc. of the Conference of the North American Chapter of the Association for Computational Linguistics: Human Language Technologies*, pages 1296–1306. DOI: 10.18653/v1/n16-1155 89

Goran Glavaš, Robert Litschko, Sebastian Ruder, and Ivan Vulić. 2019. How to (properly) evaluate cross-lingual word embeddings: On strong baselines, comparative analyses, and some misconceptions. *CoRR*, abs/1902.00508. 16, 39

Goran Glavaš and Ivan Vulić. 2018. Explicit retrofitting of distributional word vectors. In *Proc. of the 56th Annual Meeting of the Association for Computational Linguistics (Volume 1: Long Papers)*, pages 34–45. 41

Steven Gold, Anand Rangarajan, Chien-Ping Lu, Pappu Suguna, and Eric Mjolsness. 1998. New algorithms for 2D and 3D point matching:: Pose estimation and correspondence. *Pattern Recognition*, 38(8):1019–1031. DOI: 10.1016/S0031-3203(98)80010-1 70

Ian Goodfellow, Jean Pouget-Abadie, Mehdi Mirza, Bing Xu, David WardeFarley, Sherjil Ozair, Aaron Courville, and Yoshua Bengio. 2014. Generative adversarial networks. In *Proc. of the 27th Annual Conference on Neural Information Processing Systems*, pages 2672–2680. 67, 69, 70, 74

Stephan Gouws, Yoshua Bengio, and Greg Corrado. 2015. BilBOWA: Fast bilingual distributed representations without word alignments. In *Proc. of International Conference on Machine Learning*. 17, 18, 29, 50, 51, 57, 64, 86

Stephan Gouws and Anders Søgaard. 2015. Simple task-specific bilingual word embeddings. In *Proc. of North American Chapter of the Association for Computational Linguistics*. DOI: 10.3115/v1/n15-1157 14, 16, 19, 41, 44, 45, 47, 77

John C. Gower. 1975. Generalized Procrustes analysis. *Psychometrika*, 40(1):33–51. DOI: 10.1007/bf02291478 62

João Graça, Joana Paulo Pardal, Luísa Coheur, and Diamantino Caseiro. 2008. Building a golden collection of parallel multi-language word alignment. In *Proc. of the International Conference on Language Resources and Evaluation*, pages 986–993. 79

Edouard Grave, Armand Joulin, and Quentin Berthet. 2018. Unsupervised alignment of embeddings with Wasserstein Procrustes. *CoRR*, abs/1805.11222. 71, 72

Thomas L. Griffiths, Mark Steyvers, and Joshua B. Tenenbaum. 2007. Topics in semantic representation. *Psychological Review*, 114(2):211–244. DOI: 10.1037/0033-295x.114.2.211 31

Jiatao Gu, Hany Hassan, Jacob Devlin, and Victor O. K. Li. 2018a. Universal neural machine translation for extremely low resource languages. In *Proc. of the Conference of the North American Chapter of the Association for Computational Linguistics: Human Language Technologies, (Volume 1: Long Papers)*, pages 344–354. DOI: 10.18653/v1/n18-1032 79

Jiatao Gu, Yong Wang, Yun Chen, Kyunghyun Cho, and Victor O. K. Li. 2018b. Meta-learning for low-resource neural machine translation. In *Proc. of the Conference on Empirical Methods in Natural Language Processing*, pages 3622–3631. 79

Ishaan Gulrajani, Faruk Ahmed, Martin Arjovsky, Vincent Dumoulin, and Aaron Courville. 2017. Improved training of Wasserstein GANSs. In *Proc. of the 30th Annual Conference on Neural Information Processing Systems*, pages 5769–5779. 71

Jiang Guo, Wanxiang Che, David Yarowsky, Haifeng Wang, and Ting Liu. 2015. Cross-lingual dependency parsing based on distributed representations. In *Proc. of the 53rd Annual Meeting of the Association for Computational Linguistics (Volume 1: Long Papers)*, pages 1234–1244. DOI: 10.3115/v1/p15-1119 17, 19, 43, 77

Iryna Gurevych. 2005. Using the structure of a conceptual network in computing semantic relatedness. In *Proc. of the 2nd International Joint Conference on Natural Language Processing: Full Papers*. DOI: 10.1007/11562214_67 75

Michael U. Gutmann and Aapo Hyvärinen. 2012. Noise-contrastive estimation of unnormalized statistical models, with applications to natural image statistics. *Journal of Machine Learning Research*, 13(1):307–361. 11

Oussama Haddad, Julien Leboucher, Jocelyne Troccaz, and Eric Stindel. 2016. Initialized Iterative Closest Point for bone recognition in ultrasound volumes. In *Proc. of the 23rd International Conference on Pattern Recognition*, pages 2801–2806. DOI: 10.1109/icpr.2016.7900060 70

Aria Haghighi, Percy Liang, Taylor Berg-Kirkpatrick, and Dan Klein. 2008. Learning bilingual lexicons from monolingual corpora. In *Proc. of the 46th Annual Meeting of the Association for Computational Linguistics (Volume 1: Long Papers)*, pages 771–779. 26, 36

Mark Hamilton. 2018. Semi-supervised translation with MMD networks. *CoRR*, abs/1810.11906. 73

Mareike Hartmann, Yova Kementchedjhieva, and Anders Søgaard. 2018. Why is unsupervised alignment of English embeddings from different algorithms so hard? In *Proc. of the Conference on Empirical Methods in Natural Language Processing*, pages 582–586. 68, 74

Samer Hassan and Rada Mihalcea. 2009. Cross-lingual semantic relatedness using encyclopedic knowledge. In *Proc. of the Conference on Empirical Methods in Natural Language Processing*. DOI: 10.3115/1699648.1699665 75

Bradley Hauer, Garrett Nicolai, and Grzegorz Kondrak. 2017. Bootstrapping unsupervised bilingual lexicon induction. In *Proc. of the 15th Conference of the European Chapter of the Association for Computational Linguistics (Volume 2: Short Papers)*, pages 619–624. DOI: 10.18653/v1/e17-2098 16, 18, 26

Matthew Henderson, Blaise Thomson, and Steve J. Young. 2014. Robust dialog state tracking using delexicalised recurrent neural networks and unsupervised adaptation. In *Proc. of the IEEE Spoken Language Technology Workshop*, pages 360–365. DOI: 10.1109/slt.2014.7078601 21

Karl Moritz Hermann and Phil Blunsom. 2013. Multilingual distributed representations without word alignment. In *Proc. of the International Conference on Learning Representations (Conference Track)*. 17, 18, 49, 50, 52, 57

Karl Moritz Hermann and Phil Blunsom. 2014. Multilingual models for compositional distributed semantics. In *Proc. of the 52nd Annual Meeting of the Association for Computational Linguistics (Volume 1: Long Papers)*, pages 58–68. DOI: 10.3115/v1/p14-1006 14, 17, 18, 29, 32, 50, 64, 86

Martin Heusel, Hubert Ramsauer, Thomas Unterthiner, Bernhard Nessler, and Sepp Hochreiter. 2017. GANs trained by a two time-scale update rule converge to a local Nash equilibrium. In *Proc. of the 30th Annual Conference on Neural Information Processing Systems*, pages 6629–6640. 69

Geert Heyman, Ivan Vulić, and Marie-Francine Moens. 2016. C-BiLDA: Extracting cross-lingual topics from non-parallel texts by distinguishing shared from unshared content. *Data Mining and Knowledge Discovery*, 30(5):1299–1323. DOI: 10.1007/s10618-015-0442-x 31

Geert Heyman, Ivan Vulić, and Marie-Francine Moens. 2017. Bilingual lexicon induction by learning to combine word-level and character-level representations. In *Proc. of the 15th Conference of the European Chapter of the Association for Computational Linguistics (Volume 1: Long Papers)*, pages 1085–1095. DOI: 10.18653/v1/e17-1102 27

Felix Hill, Roi Reichart, and Anna Korhonen. 2015. Simlex-999: Evaluating semantic models with (genuine) similarity estimation. *Computational Linguistics*, 41(4):665–695. DOI: 10.1162/coli_a_00237 75

Thomas Hofmann. 1999. Probabilistic latent semantic indexing. In *Proc. of the 22nd Annual International ACM SIGIR Conference on Research and Development in Information Retrieval*, pages 50–57. DOI: 10.1145/312624.312649 31

Maria Holmqvist and Lars Ahrenberg. 2011. A gold standard for English–Swedish word alignment. In *Proc. of the 18th Nordic Conference of Computational Linguistics*, pages 106–113. 79

Yedid Hoshen and Lior Wolf. 2018. Non-adversarial unsupervised word translation. In *Proc. of the Conference on Empirical Methods in Natural Language Processing*, pages 469–478. 16, 38, 67, 70, 73

Eduard Hovy, Mitchell Marcus, Martha Palmer, Lance Ramshaw, and Ralph Weischedel. 2006. OntoNotes: The 90% solution. In *Proc. of the Conference of the North American Chapter of the Association for Computational Linguistics: Human Language Technologies*, pages 57–60. 77

Jagadeesh Jagarlamudi and Hal Daumé III. 2010. Extracting multilingual topics from unaligned comparable corpora. In *Proc. of the 32nd European Conference on Advances in Information Retrieval*, pages 444–456. DOI: 10.1007/978-3-642-12275-0_39 31

Heng Ji, Joel Nothman, Ben Hachey, and Radu Florian. 2015. Overview of the TAC-KBP2015 entity discovery and linking tasks. In *Proc. of the Text Analysis Conference*. 78

Anders Johannsen, Héctor Martínez Alonso, and Anders Søgaard. 2015. Any-language frame-semantic parsing. In *Proc. of the Conference on Empirical Methods in Natural Language Processing*, pages 2062–2066. DOI: 10.18653/v1/d15-1245 1, 78

Colette Joubarne and Diana Inkpen. 2011. Comparison of semantic similarity for different languages using the Google N-gram corpus and second-order co-occurrence measures. In *Proc. of the 24th Canadian Conference on Artificial Intelligence*, pages 216–221. DOI: 10.1007/978-3-642-21043-3_26 75

Armand Joulin, Piotr Bojanowski, Tomas Mikolov, Herve Jegou, and Edouard Grave. 2018. Loss in translation: Learning bilingual word mapping with a retrieval criterion. In *Proc. of the Conference on Empirical Methods in Natural Language Processing*, pages 2979–2984. 16, 39

David Kamholz, Jonathan Pool, and Susan M. Colowick. 2014. PanLex: Building a resource for panlingual lexical translation. In *Proc. of the 9th International Conference on Language Resources and Evaluation*, pages 3145–3150. 84

Yova Kementchedjhieva, Sebastian Ruder, Ryan Cotterell, and Anders Søgaard. 2018. Generalizing Procrustes analysis for better bilingual dictionary induction. In *Proc. of the 22nd Conference on Computational Natural Language Learning*, pages 211–220. 62, 63

Douwe Kiela and Stephen Clark. 2015. Multi- and cross-modal semantics beyond vision: Grounding in auditory perception. In *Proc. of the Conference on Empirical Methods in Natural Language Processing*, pages 2461–2470. DOI: 10.18653/v1/d15-1293 47

Douwe Kiela, Ivan Vulić, and Stephen Clark. 2015. Visual bilingual lexicon induction with transferred ConvNet features. In *Proc. of the Conference on Empirical Methods in Natural Language Processing*, pages 148–158. DOI: 10.18653/v1/d15-1015 14, 19, 46

Yunsu Kim, Jiahui Geng, and Hermann Ney. 2018. Improving unsupervised word-by-word translation with language model and denoising autoencoder. In *Proc. of the Conference on Empirical Methods in Natural Language Processing*, pages 862–868. 16

Alexandre Klementiev, Ivan Titov, and Binod Bhattarai. 2012. Inducing crosslingual distributed representations of words. In *Proc. of the 24th International Conference on Computational Linguistics*, pages 1459–1474. 16, 18, 32, 42, 76

Tomáš Kočiský, Karl Moritz Hermann, and Phil Blunsom. 2014. Learning bilingual word representations by marginalizing alignments. In *Proc. of the 52nd Annual Meeting of the Association for Computational Linguistics (Volume 2: Short Papers)*, pages 224–229. DOI: 10.3115/v1/p14-2037 16, 27

Philipp Koehn. 2009. *Statistical Machine Translation*. Cambridge University Press. DOI: 10.1017/cbo9780511815829 42, 79

Patrik Lambert, Adrià De Gispert, Rafael Banchs, and José B Mari no. 2005. Guidelines for word alignment evaluation and manual alignment. *Language Resources and Evaluation*, 39(4):267–285. DOI: 10.1007/s10579-005-4822-5 79

Guillaume Lample, Miguel Ballesteros, Sandeep Subramanian, Kazuya Kawakami, and Chris Dyer. 2016. Neural architectures for named entity recognition. In *Proc. of the Conference of the North American Chapter of the Association for Computational Linguistics: Human Language Technologies*, pages 260–270. DOI: 10.18653/v1/n16-1030 89

Guillaume Lample, Ludovic Denoyer, and Marc'Aurelio Ranzato. 2018a. Unsupervised machine translation using monolingual corpora only. In *Proc. of the 6th International Conference on Learning Representations*. 4, 79, 87

Guillaume Lample, Myle Ott, Alexis Conneau, Ludovic Denoyer, and Marc'Aurelio Ranzato. 2018b. Phrase-based and neural unsupervised machine translation. In *Proc. of the Conference on Empirical Methods in Natural Language Processing*, pages 5039–5049. 4, 79

Thomas K. Landauer and Susan T. Dumais. 1997. Solutions to Plato's problem: The Latent Semantic Analysis theory of acquisition, induction, and representation of knowledge. *Psychological Review*, 104(2):211–240. DOI: 10.1037//0033-295x.104.2.211 31

Adrien Lardilleux, François Yvon, and Yves Lepage. 2013. Generalizing sampling-based multilingual alignment. *Machine Translation*, 27(1):1–23. DOI: 10.1007/s10590-012-9126-0 29

Audrey Laroche and Philippe Langlais. 2010. Revisiting context-based projection methods for term-translation spotting in comparable corpora. In *Proc. of the 23rd International Conference on Computational Linguistics*, pages 617–625. 25

Stanislas Lauly, Alex Boulanger, and Hugo Larochelle. 2013. Learning multilingual word representations using a bag-of-words autoencoder. In *Proc. of the Neural Information Processing Systems Workshop on Deep Learning*. 17, 18, 50

Angeliki Lazaridou, Georgiana Dinu, and Marco Baroni. 2015. Hubness and pollution: Delving into cross-space mapping for zero-shot learning. In *Proc. of the 53rd Annual Meeting of the Association for Computational Linguistics (Volume 1: Long Papers)*, pages 270–280. DOI: 10.3115/v1/p15-1027 16, 18, 37, 40

Quoc V. Le and Tomas Mikolov. 2014. Distributed representations of sentences and documents. In *Proc. of the 31th International Conference on Machine Learning*, pages 1188–1196. 52, 57

Ira Leviant and Roi Reichart. 2015. Separated by an un-common language: Towards judgment language informed vector space modeling. *CoRR*, abs/1508.00106. 75

Omer Levy and Yoav Goldberg. 2014. Neural word embedding as implicit matrix factorization. In *Proc. of the 27th Annual Conference on Neural Information Processing Systems*, pages 2177–2185. 6, 11

Omer Levy, Yoav Goldberg, and Ido Dagan. 2015. Improving distributional similarity with lessons learned from word embeddings. *Transactions of the Association for Computational Linguistics*, 3:211–225. DOI: 10.1162/tacl_a_00134 6, 10, 11, 12, 13

Omer Levy, Anders Søgaard, and Yoav Goldberg. 2017. A strong baseline for learning cross-lingual word embeddings from sentence alignments. In *Proc. of the 15th Conference of the European Chapter of the Association for Computational Linguistics (Volume 1: Long Papers)*. DOI: 10.18653/v1/e17-1072 6, 13, 17, 18, 29, 52, 59, 64, 79

Jiwei Li and Dan Jurafsky. 2015. Do multi-sense embeddings improve natural language understanding? In *Proc. of the Conference on Empirical Methods in Natural Language Processing*, pages 1722–1732. DOI: 10.18653/v1/d15-1200 90

Percy Liang, Ben Taskar, and Dan Klein. 2006. Alignment by agreement. In *Proc. of the Conference of the North American Chapter of the Association for Computational Linguistics: Human Language Technologies*, pages 104–111. DOI: 10.3115/1220835.1220849 29

Wang Ling, Tiago Luis, Luis Marujo, Ramón Fernandez Astudillo, Silvio Amir, Chris Dyer, Alan W. Black, and Isabel Trancoso. 2015. Finding function in form: Compositional character models for open vocabulary word representation. In *Proc. of the Conference on Empirical Methods in Natural Language Processing*, pages 1520–1530. DOI: 10.18653/v1/d15-1176 89

Wang Ling, Isabel Trancoso, Chris Dyer, and Alan Black. 2016. Character-based neural machine translation. In *Proc. of the 4th International Conference on Learning Representations*. DOI: 10.18653/v1/p16-2058 89

Robert Litschko, Goran Glavaš, Simone Paolo Ponzetto, and Ivan Vulić. 2018. Unsupervised cross-lingual information retrieval using monolingual data only. In *Proc. of the 42nd Annual ACM SIGIR International Conference on Research and Development in Information Retrieval*, pages 1253–1256. DOI: 10.1145/3209978.3210157 80

Michael Littman, Susan T. Dumais, and Thomas K. Landauer. 1998. Automatic cross-language information retrieval using Latent Semantic Indexing. In Chapter 5 of *Cross-Language Information Retrieval*, pages 51–62. Kluwer Academic Publishers. DOI: 10.1007/978-1-4615-5661-9_5 31

Nikola Ljubešić and Filip Klubička. 2014. {bs,hr,sr} WaC–Web corpora of Bosnian, Croatian and Serbian. In *Proc. of the 9th Web as Corpus Workshop*, pages 29–35. DOI: 10.3115/v1/w14-0405 83

David G. Lowe. 2004. Distinctive image features from scale-invariant keypoints. *International Journal of Computer Vision*, vol. 60(2), pages 91–110. https://doi.org/10.1023/B:VISI.0000029664.99615.94 DOI: 10.1023/B:VISI.0000029664.99615.94 46

Ang Lu, Weiran Wang, Mohit Bansal, Kevin Gimpel, and Karen Livescu. 2015. Deep multilingual correlation for improved word embeddings. In *Proc. of the Conference of the North American Chapter of the Association for Computational Linguistics: Human Language Technologies*, pages 250–256. DOI: 10.3115/v1/n15-1028 16, 18, 26, 37, 53, 85

Minh-Thang Luong, Hieu Pham, and Christopher D. Manning. 2015. Bilingual word representations with monolingual quality in mind. In *Proc. of the 1st Workshop on Vector Space Modeling for Natural Language Processing*, pages 151–159. DOI: 10.3115/v1/w15-1521 17, 19, 27, 51, 52, 64, 86

Minh-Thang Luong, Richard Socher, and Christopher D. Manning. 2013. Better word representations with recursive neural networks for morphology. In *Proc. of the 17th Conference on Computational Natural Language Learning*, pages 104–113. 75

Laurens van der Maaten and Geoffrey E. Hinton. 2012. Visualizing non-metric similarities in multiple maps. *Machine Learning*, 87(1):33–55. DOI: 10.1007/s10994-011-5273-4 2

Christoph von der Malsburg. 1988. Pattern recognition by labeled graph matching. *Neural Computation*, 1(2):141–148. DOI: 10.1016/0893-6080(88)90016-0 71

William C. Mann and Sandra A. Thompson. 1988. Rhetorical structure theory: Toward a functional theory of text organization. *Interdisciplinary Journal for the Study of Discourse*, 8(3):243–281. DOI: 10.1515/text.1.1988.8.3.243 78

Ryan McDonald, Slav Petrov, and Keith Hall. 2011. Multi-source transfer of delexicalized dependency parsers. In *Proc. of the Conference on Empirical Methods in Natural Language Processing*, pages 62–72. 21, 59

Rada Mihalcea and Andras Csomai. 2007. Wikify!: Linking documents to encyclopedic knowledge. In *Proc. of the 16th ACM Conference on Information and Knowledge Management*, pages 233–242. DOI: 10.1145/1321440.1321475 78

Rada Mihalcea and Ted Pedersen. 2003.   An evaluation exercise for word alignment.   In *Proc. of the Workshop on Building and Using Parallel Texts*, pages 1–10. DOI: 10.3115/1118905.1118906 79

Tomas Mikolov, Kai Chen, Greg Corrado, and Jeffrey Dean. 2013a. Distributed representations of words and phrases and their compositionality. In *Proc. of the 27th Annual Conference on Neural Information Processing Systems*, pages 3111–3119. 1, 10, 16, 18

Tomas Mikolov, Quoc V. Le, and Ilya Sutskever. 2013b. Exploiting similarities among languages for machine translation. *CoRR*, abs/1309.4168. 14, 35, 36, 38, 42, 44, 85, 90

George A. Miller and Walter G. Charles. 1991. Contextual correlates of semantic similarity. *Language and Cognitive Processes*, 6(1):1–28. DOI: 10.1080/01690969108406936 75

David Mimno, Hanna Wallach, Jason Naradowsky, David A. Smith, and Andrew McCallum. 2009. Polylingual topic models. In *Proc. of the Conference on Empirical Methods in Natural Language Processing*, pages 880–889. DOI: 10.3115/1699571.1699627 31

Bhaskar Mitra and Nick Craswell. 2017. Neural models for information retrieval. *CoRR*, abs/1705.01509. 80

Andriy Mnih and Yee Whye Teh. 2012. A fast and simple algorithm for training neural probabilistic language models. In *Proc. of the 29th International Conference on Machine Learning*. 11

Aditya Mogadala and Achim Rettinger. 2016. Bilingual word embeddings from parallel and non-parallel corpora for cross-language text classification. In *Proc. of the Conference of the North American Chapter of the Association for Computational Linguistics: Human Language Technologies*, pages 692–702. DOI: 10.18653/v1/n16-1083 14, 17, 18, 57, 78

Nikola Mrkšić, Diarmuid Ó Séaghdha, Tsung-Hsien Wen, Blaise Thomson, and Steve Young. 2017. Neural belief tracker: Data-driven dialogue state tracking. In *Proc. of the 55th Annual Meeting of the Association for Computational Linguistics (Volume 1: Long Papers)*, pages 1777–1788. DOI: 10.18653/v1/p17-1163 16, 78

Nikola Mrkšić, Ivan Vulić, Diarmuid Ó Séaghdha, Ira Leviant, Roi Reichart, Milica Gašić, Anna Korhonen, and Steve Young. 2017. Semantic specialisation of distributional word vector spaces using monolingual and cross-lingual constraints. *Transactions of the Association for Computational Linguistics*, 5:309–324. DOI: 10.1162/tacl_a_00063 18, 21, 40, 59, 75, 78

Youssef Mroueh and Tom Sercu. 2017. Fisher GAN. In *Proc. of the 30th Annual Conference on Neural Information Processing Systems*, pages 2510–2520. 70

Tanmoy Mukherjee, Makoto Yamada, and Timothy Hospedales. 2018. Learning unsupervised word translations without adversaries. In *Proc. of the Conference on Empirical Methods in Natural Language Processing*, pages 627–632. 16

Dragos Stefan Munteanu and Daniel Marcu. 2006. Extracting parallel sub-sentential fragments from non-parallel corpora. In *Proc. of the 44th Annual Meeting of the Association for Computational Linguistics*, pages 81–88. DOI: 10.3115/1220175.1220186 14

Rudra Murthy, Mitesh Khapra, and Pushpak Bhattacharyya. 2016. Sharing network parameters for crosslingual named entity recognition. *CoRR*, abs/1607.00198. 77

Vaishnavh Nagarajan and J. Zico Kolter. 2017. Gradient descent GAN optimization is locally stable. In *Proc. of the 30th Annual Conference on Neural Information Processing Systems*, pages 5591–5600. 69

Ndapa Nakashole. 2018. NORMA: Neighborhood sensitive maps for multilingual word embeddings. In *Proc. of the Conference on Empirical Methods in Natural Language Processing*, pages 512–522. 16

Ndapa Nakashole and Raphael Flauger. 2018. Characterizing departures from linearity in word translation. In *Proc. of the 56th Annual Meeting of the Association for Computational Linguistics (Volume 2: Short Papers)*, pages 221–227. 68, 74, 91

Ndapandula Nakashole and Raphael Flauger. 2017. Knowledge distillation for bilingual dictionary induction. In *Proc. of the Conference on Empirical Methods in Natural Language Processing*, pages 2497–2506. DOI: 10.18653/v1/d17-1264 16

Tahira Naseem, Benjamin Snyder, Jacob Eisenstein, and Regina Barzilay. 2009. Multilingual part-of-speech tagging: Two unsupervised approaches. *Journal of Artificial Intelligence Research*, 36:341–385. DOI: 10.1613/jair.2843 59

Roberto Navigli and Simone Paolo Ponzetto. 2012. BabelNet: The automatic construction, evaluation and application of a wide-coverage multilingual semantic network. *Artificial Intelligence*, 193:217–250. DOI: 10.1016/j.artint.2012.07.001 84

Joakim Nivre, Marie-Catherine de Marneffe, Filip Ginter, Yoav Goldberg, Jan Hajic, Christopher D. Manning, Ryan T McDonald, Slav Petrov, Sampo Pyysalo, Natalia Silveira, et al. 2016. Universal Dependencies v1: A multilingual treebank collection. In *Proc. of the 10th International Conference on Language Resources and Evaluation*, pages 1659–1666. 77

Franz Josef Och. 1999. An efficient method for determining bilingual word classes. In *Proc. of the 9th Conference of the European Chapter of the Association for Computational Linguistics*, pages 71–76. DOI: 10.3115/977035.977046 23

Franz Josef Och and Hermann Ney. 2003. A systematic comparison of various statistical alignment models. *Computational Linguistics*, 29(1):19–51. DOI: 10.1162/089120103321337421 27, 28

Prakhar Pandey, Vikram Pudi, and Masnish Shrivastava. 2017. Injecting word embeddings with another language's resource: An application of bilingual embeddings. In *Proc. of the 8th International Joint Conference on Natural Language Processing (Volume 2: Short Papers)*, pages 116–121. 41

Yves Peirsman and Sebastian Padó. 2010. Cross-lingual induction of selectional preferences with bilingual vector spaces. In *Proc. of the Conference of the North American Chapter of the Association for Computational Linguistics: Human Language Technologies*, pages 921–929. 26

Yves Peirsman and Sebastian Padó. 2011. Semantic relations in bilingual lexicons. *ACM Transactions on Speech and Language Processing*, 8(2):3. DOI: 10.1145/2050100.2050102 39

Jeffrey Pennington, Richard Socher, and Christopher D. Manning. 2014. Glove: Global vectors for word representation. In *Proc. of Empirical Methods in Natural Language Processing*. DOI: 10.3115/v1/d14-1162 1, 11

Hieu Pham, Minh-Thang Luong, and Christopher D. Manning. 2015. Learning distributed representations for multilingual text sequences. In *Proc. of the 1st Workshop on Vector Space Modeling for Natural Language Processing*, pages 88–94. DOI: 10.3115/v1/w15-1512 17, 52, 57

John C. Platt, Kristina Toutanova, and Wen-Tau Yih. 2010. Translingual document representations from discriminative projections. In *Proc. of the Conference on Empirical Methods in Natural Language Processing*, pages 251–261. 31

Edoardo Maria Ponti, Ivan Vulić, Goran Glavaš, Nikola Mrkšić, and Anna Korhonen. 2018. Adversarial propagation and zero-shot cross-lingual transfer of word vector specialization. In *Proc. of the Conference on Empirical Methods in Natural Language Processing*, pages 282–293. 41

Peter Prettenhofer and Benno Stein. 2010. Cross-language text classification using structural correspondence learning. In *Proc. of the 48th Annual Meeting of the Association for Computational Linguistics*, pages 1118–1127. 78

Miloš Radovanović, Alexandros Nanopoulos, and Mirjana Ivanović. 2010. Hubs in space: Popular nearest neighbors in high-dimensional data. *Journal of Machine Learning Research*, 11:2487–2531. 34, 71

Janarthanan Rajendran, Mitesh M. Khapra, Sarath Chandar, and Balaraman Ravindran. 2016. Bridge correlational neural networks for multilingual multimodal representation learning. In *Proc. of the Conference of the North American Chapter of the Association for Computational Linguistics: Human Language Technologies*, pages 171–181. DOI: 10.18653/v1/n16-1021 17, 18, 52

Reinhard Rapp. 1999. Automatic identification of word translations from unrelated English and German corpora. In *Proc. of the 37th Annual Meeting of the Association for Computational Linguistics*, pages 519–526. DOI: 10.3115/1034678.1034756 25

Guy Rotman, Ivan Vulić, and Roi Reichart. 2018. Bridging languages through images with Deep Partial Canonical Correlation Analysis. In *Proc. of the 56th Annual Meeting of the Association for Computational Linguistics (Volume 1: Long Papers)*, pages 910–921. 17, 85

Herbert Rubenstein and John B. Goodenough. 1965. Contextual correlates of synonymy. *Communications of the ACM*, 8(10):627–633. DOI: 10.1145/365628.365657 75

Sebastian Ruder, Ryan Cotterell, Yova Kementchedjhieva, and Anders Søgaard. 2018. A Discriminative Latent-Variable Model for Bilingual Lexicon Induction. In *Proc. of Empirical Methods in Natural Language Processing*. 16, 27, 39, 85

Tobias Schnabel, Igor Labutov, David Mimno, and Thorsten Joachims. 2015. Evaluation methods for unsupervised word embeddings. In *Proc. of the Conference on Empirical Methods in Natural Language Processing*, pages 298–307. DOI: 10.18653/v1/d15-1036 75

Peter H. Schönemann. 1966. A generalized solution of the orthogonal Procrustes problem. *Psychometrika*, 31(1):1–10. DOI: 10.1007/bf02289451 57, 67

Tanja Schultz and Alex Waibel. 2001. Language-independent and language-adaptive acoustic modeling for speech recognition. *Speech Communication*, 35(1):31–51. DOI: 10.1016/s0167-6393(00)00094-7 21

Rico Sennrich, Barry Haddow, and Alexandra Birch. 2016. Neural machine translation of rare words with subword units. In *Proc. of the 54th Annual Meeting of the Association for Computational Linguistics (Volume 1: Long Papers)*, pages 1715–1725. DOI: 10.18653/v1/p16-1162 89

Serge Sharoff. 2006. A uniform interface to large-scale linguistic resources. In *Proc. of the 5th International Conference on Language Resources and Evaluation*, pages 539–542. 83

Daphna Shezaf and Ari Rappoport. 2010. Bilingual lexicon generation using non-aligned signatures. In *Proc. of the 48th Annual Meeting of the Association for Computational Linguistics*, pages 98–107. 52

Tianze Shi, Zhiyuan Liu, Yang Liu, and Maosong Sun. 2015. Learning cross-lingual word embeddings via matrix co-factorization. In *Proc. of the 53rd Annual Meeting of the Association for Computational Linguistics (Volume 2: Short Papers)*, pages 567–572. DOI: 10.3115/v1/p15-2093 17, 18, 42

Samuel L. Smith, David H. P. Turban, Steven Hamblin, and Nils Y. Hammerla. 2017. Offline bilingual word vectors, orthogonal transformations and the inverted softmax. In *Proc. of the 5th International Conference on Learning Representations*. 2, 16, 18, 36, 38, 39, 60, 67, 85

Benjamin Snyder and Regina Barzilay. 2010. Climbing the tower of Babel: Unsupervised multilingual learning. In *Proc. of the 27th International Conference on Machine Learning*, pages 29–36. 59

Anders Søgaard. 2011. Data point selection for cross-language adaptation of dependency parsers. In *Proc. of the 49th Annual Meeting of the Association for Computational Linguistics: Human Language Technologies*, pages 682–686. 21

Anders Søgaard. 2016. Evaluating word embeddings with FMRI and eye-tracking. In *Proc. of the 1st Workshop on Evaluating Vector-Space Representations for NLP*, pages 116–121. DOI: 10.18653/v1/w16-2521 47, 80

Anders Søgaard, Željko Agić, Héctor Martíney Alonso, Barbara Plank, Bernd Bohnet, and Anders Johannsen. 2015. Inverted indexing for cross-lingual NLP. In *Proc. of the 53rd Annual Meeting of the Association for Computational Linguistics*, pages 1713–1722. DOI: 10.3115/v1/p15-1165 17, 18, 56, 64

Anders Søgaard, Sebastian Ruder, and Ivan Vulić. 2018. On the limitations of unsupervised bilingual dictionary induction. In *Proc. of Association for Computational Linguistics*, pages 778–788. 38, 67, 69, 74, 91

Hubert Soyer, Pontus Stenetorp, and Akiko Aizawa. 2015. Leveraging monolingual data for crosslingual compositional word representations. In *Proc. of the 3rd International Conference on Learning Representations*. 17, 18, 50, 64

Oscar Täckström, Ryan McDonald, and Jakob Uszkoreit. 2012. Cross-lingual word clusters for direct transfer of linguistic structure. In *Proc. of the Conference of the North American Chapter of the Association for Computational Linguistics: Human Language Technologies*, pages 477–487. 21, 23, 24, 32, 77

Akihiro Tamura, Taro Watanabe, and Eiichiro Sumita. 2012. Bilingual lexicon extraction from comparable corpora using label propagation. In *Proc. of the Joint Conference on Empirical Methods in Natural Language Processing and Computational Natural Language Learning*, pages 24–36. 25

Jörg Tiedemann. 2012. Parallel data, tools and interfaces in OPUS. In *Proc. of the 8th International Conference on Language Resources and Evaluation*, pages 2214–2218. 84

Erik F. Tjong Kim Sang and Fien De Meulder. 2002. Introduction to the CoNLL-2002 shared task: Language-independent named entity recognition, proceedings of the 6th conference on natural language learning. In *Proc. of the 6th Conference on Natural Language Learning*. DOI: 10.3115/1119176.1119195 77

Erik F. Tjong Kim Sang and Fien De Meulder. 2003. Introduction to the CoNLL-2003 shared task: Language-independent named entity recognition. In *Proc. of the 7th Conference on Natural Language Learning*, pages 142–147. DOI: 10.3115/1119176.1119195 77

Chen-Tse Tsai and Dan Roth. 2016. Cross-lingual wikification using multilingual embeddings. In *Proc. of the Conference of the North American Chapter of the Association for Computational Linguistics: Human Language Technologies*, pages 589–598. DOI: 10.18653/v1/n16-1072 78

Yulia Tsvetkov, Manaal Faruqui, Wang Ling, Guillaume Lample, and Chris Dyer. 2015. Evaluation of word vector representations by subspace alignment. In *Proc. of the Conference on Empirical Methods in Natural Language Processing*, pages 2049–2054. DOI: 10.18653/v1/d15-1243 76

Yulia Tsvetkov, Sunayana Sitaram, Manaal Faruqui, Guillaume Lample, Patrick Littell, David Mortensen, Alan W. Black, Lori Levin, and Chris Dyer. 2016. Polyglot neural language models: A case study in cross-lingual phonetic representation learning. In *Proc. of the Conference of the North American Chapter of the Association for Computational Linguistics: Human Language Technologies*, pages 1357–1366. DOI: 10.18653/v1/n16-1161 75

Joseph Turian, Lev Ratinov, and Yoshua Bengio. 2010. Word representations: A simple and general method for semi-supervised learning. In *Proc. of the 48th Annual Meeting of the Association for Computational Linguistics*, pages 384–394. 80

Peter D. Turney and Patrick Pantel. 2010. From frequency to meaning: Vector space models of semantics. *Journal of Artificial Intelligence Research*, 37:141–188. DOI: 10.1613/jair.2934 26

Shyam Upadhyay, Manaal Faruqui, Chris Dyer, and Dan Roth. 2016. Cross-lingual models of word embeddings: An empirical comparison. In *Proc. of the 54th Annual Meeting of the Association for Computational Linguistics (Volume 1: Long Papers)*, pages 1661–1670. DOI: 10.18653/v1/p16-1157 6, 13, 77, 79, 87

Jakob Uszkoreit and Thorsten Brants. 2008. Distributed word clustering for large scale class-based language modeling in machine translation. In *Proc. of the 46th Annual Meeting of the Association for Computational Linguistics*, pages 755–762. 23

Ivan Vulić, Wim De Smet, and Marie-Francine Moens. 2011. Identifying word translations from comparable corpora using latent topic models. In *Proc. of the 49th Annual Meeting of the Association for Computational Linguistics: Human Language Technologies*, pages 479–484. 31, 57

Ivan Vulić, Wim De Smet, Jie Tang, and Marie-Francine Moens. 2015. Probabilistic topic modeling in multilingual settings: An overview of its methodology and applications. *Information Processing and Management*, 51(1):111–147. DOI: 10.1016/j.ipm.2014.08.003 29, 31, 72

Ivan Vulić, Goran Glavaš, Nikola Mrkšić, and Anna Korhonen. 2018. Post-specialisation: Retrofitting vectors of words unseen in lexical resources. In *Proc. of the Conference of the North American Chapter of the Association for Computational Linguistics: Human Language Technologies (Volume 1: Long Papers)*, pages 516–527. DOI: 10.18653/v1/n18-1048 41

Ivan Vulić, Douwe Kiela, Stephen Clark, and Marie-Francine Moens. 2016. Multi-modal representations for improved bilingual lexicon learning. In *Proc. of the 54th Annual Meeting of the Association for Computational Linguistics (Volume 2: Short Papers)*, pages 188–194. DOI: 10.18653/v1/p16-2031 19, 46, 64

Ivan Vulić and Anna Korhonen. 2016. On the role of seed lexicons in learning bilingual word embeddings. In *Proc. of the 54th Annual Meeting of the Association for Computational Linguistics (Volume 1: Long Papers)*, pages 247–257. DOI: 10.18653/v1/p16-1024 16, 19, 39, 85

Ivan Vulić and Marie-Francine Moens. 2012. Sub-corpora sampling with an application to bilingual lexicon extraction. In *Proc. of the 24th International Conference on Computational Linguistics*, pages 2721–2738. 29

Ivan Vulić and Marie-Francine Moens. 2013. Cross-lingual semantic similarity of words as the similarity of their semantic word responses. In *Proc. of the Conference of the North American Chapter of the Association for Computational Linguistics: Human Language Technologies*, pages 106–116. 17, 19, 56

Ivan Vulić and Marie-Francine Moens. 2013. A study on bootstrapping bilingual vector spaces from non-parallel data (and nothing else). In *Proc. of the Conference on Empirical Methods in Natural Language Processing*, pages 1613–1624. 14, 26, 39

Ivan Vulić and Marie-Francine Moens. 2015. Monolingual and cross-lingual information retrieval models based on (bilingual) word embeddings. In *Proc. of the 38th Annual International*

ACM SIGIR Conference on Research and Development in Information Retrieval, pages 363–372. DOI: 10.1145/2766462.2767752 17, 80

Ivan Vulić and Marie-Francine Moens. 2016. Bilingual distributed word representations from document-aligned comparable data. *Journal of Artificial Intelligence Research*, 55:953–994. DOI: 10.1613/jair.4986 17, 19, 55, 56, 67, 86

Yogarshi Vyas and Marine Carpuat. 2016. Sparse bilingual word representations for cross-lingual lexical entailment. In *Proc. of the Conference of the North American Chapter of the Association for Computational Linguistics: Human Language Technologies*, pages 1187–1197. DOI: 10.18653/v1/n16-1142 17, 18, 42

Zhichun Wang, Qingsong Lv, Xiaohan Lan, and Yu Zhang. 2018. Cross-lingual knowledge graph alignment via graph convolutional networks. In *Proc. of the Conference on Empirical Methods in Natural Language Processing*, pages 349–357. 71

Xiang Wei, Boqing Gong, Zixia Liu, Wei Lu, and Liqiang Wang. 2018. Improving the improved training of Wasserstain GANs: A consistency term and its dual effect. In *Proc. of the 6th International Conference on Learning Representations*. 71

Tsung-Hsien Wen, David Vandyke, Nikola Mrkšić, Milica Gašić, Lina M Rojas-Barahona, Pei-Hao Su, Stefan Ultes, and Steve Young. 2017. A network-based end-to-end trainable task-oriented dialogue system. In *Proc. of the 15th Conference of the European Chapter of the Association for Computational Linguistics (Volume 1: Long Papers)*, pages 438–449. DOI: 10.18653/v1/e17-1042 78

Michael Wick, Pallika Kanani, and Adam Pocock. 2016. Minimally-constrained multilingual embeddings via artificial code-switching. In *Proc. of the 30th AAAI Conference on Artificial Intelligence*, pages 2849–2855. 41

John Wieting, Mohit Bansal, Kevin Gimpel, and Karen Livescu. 2015. From paraphrase database to compositional paraphrase model and back. *Transactions of the Association for Computational Linguistics*, 3:345–358. DOI: 10.1162/tacl_a_00143 40

Derry Tanti Wijaya, Brendan Callahan, John Hewitt, Jie Gao, Xiao Ling, Marianna Apidianaki, and Chris Callison-Burch. 2017. Learning translations via matrix completion. In *Proc. of the Conference on Empirical Methods in Natural Language Processing*, pages 1452–1463. DOI: 10.18653/v1/d17-1152 16, 79

Min Xiao and Yuhong Guo. 2014. Distributed word representation learning for cross-lingual dependency parsing. In *Proc. of the 18th Conference on Computational Natural Language Learning*, pages 119–129. DOI: 10.3115/v1/w14-1613 16, 19, 41, 44, 45

Chao Xing, Dong Wang, Chao Liu, and Yiye Lin. 2015. Normalized word embedding and orthogonal transform for bilingual word translation. In *Proc. of the Conference of the North American Chapter of the Association for Computational Linguistics: Human Language Technologies*, pages 1006–1011. DOI: 10.3115/v1/n15-1104 16, 18, 36

Ruochen Xu, Yiming Yang, Naoki Otani, and Yuexin Wu. 2018. Unsupervised cross-lingual transfer of word embedding spaces. In *Proc. of the Conference on Empirical Methods in Natural Language Processing*, pages 2465–2474. 16, 71, 73

Jiaolong Yang, Hongdong Li, Dylan Campbell, and Yunde Jia. 2016. Go-ICP: A globally optimal solution to 3D ICP point-set registration. *IEEE Transactions on Pattern Analysis and Machine Intelligence*, 38(11):2241–2254. DOI: 10.1109/tpami.2015.2513405 70

Zhen Yang, Wei Chen, Feng Wang, and Bo Xu. 2018. Unsupervised neural machine translation with weight sharing. In *Proc. of the 56th Annual Meeting of the Association for Computational Linguistics (Volume 1: Long Papers)*, pages 46–55. 73, 79

Yuya Yoshikawa, Tomoharu Iwata, Hiroshi Sawada, and Takeshi Yamada. 2015. Cross-domain matching for bag-of-words data via kernel embeddings of latent distributions. In *Proc. of the 28th Annual Conference on Neural Information Processing Systems*, pages 1405–1413. 73

Hamed Zamani and W. Bruce Croft. 2016. Embedding-based query language models. In *Proc. of the ACM on International Conference on the Theory of Information Retrieval*, pages 147–156. DOI: 10.1145/2970398.2970405 80

Daniel Zeman, Martin Popel, Milan Straka, Jan Hajic, Joakim Nivre, Filip Ginter, Juhani Luotolahti, Sampo Pyysalo, Slav Petrov, Martin Potthast, Francis Tyers, Elena Badmaeva, Memduh Gokirmak, Anna Nedoluzhko, Silvie Cinkova, Jan Hajic jr., Jaroslava Hlavacova, Václava Kettnerová, Zdenka Uresova, Jenna Kanerva, Stina Ojala, Anna Missilä, Christopher D. Manning, Sebastian Schuster, Siva Reddy, Dima Taji, Nizar Habash, Herman Leung, Marie-Catherine de Marneffe, Manuela Sanguinetti, Maria Simi, Hiroshi Kanayama, Valeria dePaiva, Kira Droganova, Héctor Martínez Alonso, Çağrı Çöltekin, Umut Sulubacak, Hans Uszkoreit, Vivien Macketanz, Aljoscha Burchardt, Kim Harris, Katrin Marheinecke, Georg Rehm, Tolga Kayadelen, Mohammed Attia, Ali Elkahky, Zhuoran Yu, Emily Pitler, Saran Lertpradit, Michael Mandl, Jesse Kirchner, Hector Fernandez Alcalde, Jana Strnadová, Esha Banerjee, Ruli Manurung, Antonio Stella, Atsuko Shimada, Sookyoung Kwak, Gustavo Mendonca, Tatiana Lando, Rattima Nitisaroj, and Josie Li. 2017. CoNLL 2017 Shared Task: Multilingual parsing from raw text to Universal Dependencies. In *Proc. of the CoNLL Shared Task: Multilingual Parsing from Raw Text to Universal Dependencies*, pages 1–19. DOI: 10.18653/v1/k17-3001 21

Daniel Zeman and Philip Resnik. 2008. Cross-language parser adaptation between related languages. In *Proc. of the Workshop on NLP for Less Privileged Languages*. 21

Duo Zhang, Qiaozhu Mei, and ChengXiang Zhai. 2010. Cross-lingual latent topic extraction. In *Proc. of the 48th Annual Meeting of the Association for Computational Linguistics*, pages 1128–1137. 31

Meng Zhang, Yang Liu, Huanbo Luan, Yiqun Liu, and Maosong Sun. 2016a. Inducing bilingual lexica from non-parallel data with Earth mover's distance regularization. In *Proc. of the 26th International Conference on Computational Linguistics (Technical Papers)*, pages 3188–3198. 16, 18, 91

Meng Zhang, Yang Liu, Huanbo Luan, and Maosong Sun. 2017a. Adversarial training for unsupervised bilingual lexicon induction. In *Proc. of the 55th Annual Meeting of the Association for Computational Linguistics (Volume 1: Long Papers)*, pages 1959–1970. DOI: 10.18653/v1/p17-1179 16, 36, 68, 70, 91

Meng Zhang, Yang Liu, Huanbo Luan, and Maosong Sun. 2017b. Earth mover's distance minimization for unsupervised bilingual lexicon induction. In *Proc. of the Conference on Empirical Methods in Natural Language Processing*, pages 1934–1945. DOI: 10.18653/v1/d17-1207 16, 91

Yuan Zhang, David Gaddy, Regina Barzilay, and Tommi Jaakkola. 2016b. Ten Pairs to Tag–Multilingual POS tagging via coarse mapping between embeddings. In *Proc. of the Conference of the North American Chapter of the Association for Computational Linguistics: Human Language Technologies*, pages 1307–1317. DOI: 10.18653/v1/n16-1156 36, 77

Will Y. Zou, Richard Socher, Daniel Cer, and Christopher D. Manning. 2013. Bilingual word embeddings for phrase-based machine translation. In *Proc. of the Conference on Empirical Methods in Natural Language Processing*, pages 1393–1398. 17, 18, 23, 64, 77, 79

Authors' Biographies

ANDERS SØGAARD

Anders Søgaard is a Professor in Computer Science of the University of Copenhagen. He is funded by a Google Focused Research Award, and before that, he held an ERC Starting Grant. He has won best paper awards at NAACL, EACL, CoNLL, and more. He is interested in the learnability of language.

IVAN VULIĆ

Ivan Vulić is a Senior Research Associate in the Language Technology Lab at the University of Cambridge since 2015. Ivan holds a Ph.D. in Computer Science from KU Leuven, having achieved summa cum laude in 2014 on "Unsupervised Algorithms for Cross-lingual Text Analysis, Translation Mining, and Information Retrieval." He is interested in representation learning, human language understanding, distributional, lexical, and multi-modal semantics in monolingual and multilingual contexts, and transfer learning for enabling cross-lingual NLP applications. He has co-authored more than 60 peer-reviewed research papers published in top-tier journals and conference proceedings in NLP and IR. He co-lectured a tutorial on monolingual and multilingual topic models and applications at ECIR 2013 and WSDM 2014, a tutorial on word vector space specialisation at EACL 2017 and ESSLLI 2018, a tutorial on cross-lingual word representations at EMNLP 2017, and a tutorial on deep learning for conversational AI at NAACL 2018.

SEBASTIAN RUDER

Sebastian Ruder is a Research Scientist at DeepMind. He obtained his Ph.D. in Natural Language Processing at the National University of Ireland, Galway in 2019. He is interested in transfer learning and cross-lingual learning and has published widely read reviews as well as more than ten peer-reviewed research papers in top-tier conference proceedings in NLP.

MANAAL FARUQUI

Manaal Faruqui is a Senior Research Scientist at Google, working on industrial scale NLP and ML problems. He obtained his Ph.D. in the Language Technologies Institute at Carnegie Mellon University while working on representation learning, multilingual learning, and distributional and lexical semantics. He received a best paper award at NAACL 2015 for his work on incorporating semantic knowledge in word vector representations. He serves on the editorial board of the *Computational Linguistics* journal and has been an area chair for several ACL conferences.

Printed in the United States
by Baker & Taylor Publisher Services